Illuminating Literature:
When Worlds Collide
—— Teacher's Guide ——

Sharon Watson

Writing with Sharon Watson

ISBN-13: 978-1512158649

ISBN-10: 151215864X

Special thanks to Esther Moulder of ClickPhotography.biz for the lovely cover photo and to research assistant Hannah Ihms for letting me borrow her elegant mind.

Writing with Sharon Watson
Illuminating Literature: When Worlds Collide

WritingWithSharonWatson.com

Illuminating Literature: When Worlds Collide

For Christian High Schools, Homeschools, and Co-ops

Teacher's Guide

Sharon Watson

WritingWithSharonWatson.com

Companion books in this series:

Illuminating Literature: When Worlds Collide, student textbook

Illuminating Literature: When Worlds Collide,
Quiz and Answer Manual

Illuminating Literature: When Worlds Collide, Novel Notebook
(Download this FREE at http://writingwithsharonwatson.com/illuminating-
literature-when-worlds-collide-gateway/.)

The approved bundle of eight books students read in this course is available at
http://writingwithsharonwatson.com/illuminating-literature-when-worlds-collide/.

Also by Sharon Watson:

Jump In, middle school writing curriculum published by Apologia and
featured in Cathy Duffy's *102 Top Picks for Homeschool Curriculum.*
"*Jump In* . . . has revolutionized the way we learn writing,
literally one skill at a time." –Heather, mom
http://writingwithsharonwatson.com/jump-in/

The Power in Your Hands: Writing Nonfiction in High School
"The dread is dead and my son is loving this course!"
–Kathy D., homeschoolbuzz.com
http://writingwithsharonwatson.com/the-power-in-your-hands/

Writing Fiction [in High School]
"This course was one of the most entertaining and useful classes I took all
year, if not one of my favorites from my entire high school career."
–Phillip, senior

http://writingwithsharonwatson.com/writing-fiction-in-high-school/

WritingWithSharonWatson.com

Approved versions of the books read in this course:

Title and Author	Publisher	ISBN
Pudd'nhead Wilson by Mark Twain	(Dover Publications)	0-486-40885-X
The War of the Worlds by H. G. Wells	(Dover Publications)	0-486-29506-0
The Friendly Persuasion by Jessamyn West	(Harcourt, Inc.)	0-15-602909-X or 0-15-633606-5
Peter Pan by Sir James Barrie	(Dover Publications)	0-486-40783-7
Warriors Don't Cry by Melba Pattillo Beals	(Washington Square Press/Pocket Books)	0-671-86639-7
A Tale of Two Cities by Charles Dickens	(Dover Publications)	0-486-40651-2
Fahrenheit 451 by Ray Bradbury	(Simon & Schuster)	978-1-4516-7331-9
The Screwtape Letters by C. S. Lewis	(HarperCollins)	978-0-06-065293-7

The approved bundle of eight books students read in this course is available at http://writingwithsharonwatson.com/illuminating-literature-when-worlds-collide/.

Why use the approved bundle? All page numbers referenced in the textbook are from the approved versions of each book. Students who do not have the approved version of each novel will become discouraged trying to find the passages and will learn less than their peers.

Students reading the books from a tablet will be able to keep up if they know how to use the Search function.

Table of Contents

About This Course: Welcome, Teacher!

Welcome to a wonderful year of illuminating literature!

You'll find important information on these first pages before the answer key. Please take a few moments to read them.

This year, your students will become

- more knowledgeable and discerning readers and
- more powerful fiction writers.

This course makes a literature class possible for you and your teens and makes difficult concepts easy for students to understand in a relaxed atmosphere.

Each book below was selected for its colliding worlds, its literary value, and for its potential to help students make moral, ethical, spiritual, and life choices from a godly perspective.

While *Illuminating Literature: When Worlds Collide* is written from a Christian perspective and respects the Bible as the ultimate source of truth, the individual authors of this year's list of books may or may not be self-described Christians. The material found in the individual books will reflect the authors' worldviews and may occasionally contain words, characters, or events that may be offensive to some readers. However, your students will learn this year how to analyze stories to sort the wheat from the chaff.

The Books

Below is the list of books your students will be reading, along with the suggested publisher and the ISBN. **It is highly recommended that your students use the suggested version of each book.**

All page numbers in this teacher's guide and in the student's textbook are from those versions. This makes following along EASY.

Title and Author	(Publisher)	ISBN
Pudd'nhead Wilson by Mark Twain	(Dover Publications)	0-486-40885-X
The War of the Worlds by H. G. Wells	(Dover Publications)	0-486-29506-0
The Friendly Persuasion by Jessamyn West	(Harcourt, Inc.)	0-15-602909-X
		or 0-15-633606-5
Peter Pan by Sir James Barrie	(Dover Publications)	0-486-40783-7
Warriors Don't Cry by Melba Pattillo Beals	(Washington Square Press/Pocket Books)	
		0-671-86639-7
A Tale of Two Cities by Charles Dickens	(Dover Publications)	0-486-40651-2
Fahrenheit 451 by Ray Bradbury	(Simon & Schuster)	978-1-4516-7331-9
The Screwtape Letters by C. S. Lewis	(HarperCollins)	978-0-06-065293-7

Note: There is a cheaper version of *Warriors Don't Cry* with a red cover and a black-and-white photo of some of the students moving from the school to the station wagon, with soldiers in the background. This version, however, is abridged and will not match the page numbers referred to in this course.

The one deviation from the list that I allow in my literature classes is when a student uses Kindle, NOOK, or some other tablet that has a search function that the student knows how to use. Students using these devices and the search function keep up in class nicely and can track with the written material in the textbook.

Warning: Avoid this Potential Disaster.

I've taught literature classes where some of the students did not have the suggested version of each book, and the result was chaotic. Students who used books from the library or from home were lost as we turned to specific pages and passages because the material in their books did not appear on the same pages as in our books. They spent so much time trying to keep up that they became frustrated and learned less than their peers did.

Grades

Grading will be easy for you this year. In fact, some of it will be done for you as your students complete free online quizzes. Links to all online quizzes can be found at http://WritingWithSharonWatson.com/illuminating-literature-when-worlds-collide-gateway/. Grades for each book will be based on the following:

- Online "Yes, I read it" quiz, graded online (1-10 points)
- Online literary terms quiz, graded online (1-10 points)
- Participation in opinion survey online (1-10 points)
- Quality of participation in discussions (1-20 points)
- Successful completion of lessons and assignments (1-20 points)
- Successful completion of activities (1-10 points)
- Completion of each book on the book list (1-20 points)

You'll find a **grading grid** on the next page, marked for a possible 100 points per book. This grid will be placed at the end of each chapter in this answer key and labeled with the current book's title. Please feel free to adjust each grid to your needs and expectations.

Opinion surveys have no correct answer; students are graded on participation. Their answers to the opinion surveys may help you develop a strategy for your discussion time.

You have permission to copy each grading grid as many times as needed for your own class, co-op, reading group, book-of-the-month club, or family.

If you prefer that students take the quizzes on paper, you'll need *Illuminating Literature: When Worlds Collide, Quiz and Answer Key*, available for sale at http://writingwithsharonwatson.com/illuminating-literature-when-worlds-collide-gateway/.

Grading Grid

Online "Yes, I read it" quiz, graded online. 1-10 points	
Online literary terms quiz, graded online. 1-10 points	
Participation in opinion questions online. 1-10 points	
Quality of participation in discussions. 1-20 points	
Successful completion of lessons and assignments. 1-20 points	
Successful completion of activity. 1-10 points	
Finished reading the book. 1-20 points.	
Total grade for current book	

Writing with Sharon Watson

4

Course Objectives

Objectives for each chapter appear in that chapter's answer key. Objectives for the whole course are as follows:

Skills

To teach literary terms and writers' devices.
To teach story elements such as setting, characterization, and point of view.
To improve vocabulary by giving Vocabulary Quizzolas.
To give students a chance to prove they read each book by completing the online multiple-choice "Yes, I read it" quiz.
To reinforce literary terms with online quizzes.
To develop powerful fiction writers through writing exercises.
To help students understand conflict in books and, therefore, in life.
To develop discerning and savvy readers.
To understand what the author does to mold their hearts.

Attitude

To engender a love of fine literature.
To make it possible for those who do not like reading or might not have participated in literature classes to be successful and thrive in one.
To delight students who already love literature classes by showing them the beauties of the novels and of the English language.
To avoid sucking the life out of the class due to wringing out each novel until it begs for mercy.

Course

To provide a two-semester literature class for language arts requirements.
To provide a safe place where students can discuss the grand themes and spiritual, ethical, moral, cultural, and personal topics in these novels.
To give students a chance to participate in group activities.
To allow students to express their opinions and interpretations in non-graded multiple-choice questions online.
To interpret these novels from a balanced perspective, not just from a socio-economic, political, racial, or gender-based perspective.
To provide activities that fit a number of learning styles.
To examine literature in a relaxed atmosphere.
To view literature through the lens of the truths found in the Bible.

Alone or in a Group?

This course can be completed by the self-guided homeschool student with very little input from the teacher. It can also be used in a co-op, a reading group you develop for your students, or a classroom setting. Students will benefit the most from the discussions and group activities if they have a group to participate with, of course.

The course is developed from reading groups I taught called Book-of-the-Month Clubs in which students read a book of the month and then discussed it. You may do the same, if you wish, or devise your own method of meeting as a group.

Beginning at the bottom of this page, you'll find a suggested schedule for conducting a once-a-month class.

Whether you choose to meet weekly, every other week, or monthly, you'll be giving your students a lasting gift of a love for fine literature and an understanding of some of the grander themes of human existence. And students will have a much clearer understanding of how the author molds their heart!

Facebook Group

If you lead a group, you may want to create a secret Facebook group for only your students and their parents. This way, you can discuss issues or ask questions of the students on the weeks you don't meet. In each chapter, I'll include specific questions and links I've used in my Facebook group.

The Novel Notebook

Your students will need an empty notebook that we'll call the Novel Notebook. This notebook can be spiral bound, loose papers in a three-ring binder, or a file on their computer. They will be instructed to look for certain things in the novels and make a note of them in their Novel Notebook. They'll also be looking for especially well-written or poorly written passages so they can learn from those. After they've read each novel, they will use their Novel Notebook to answer some questions. Make sure they have one at the beginning of the course.

If you would you like a **FREE 101-page Novel Notebook** with the questions and journaling questions already in it, download Novel Notebooks for students here: http://writingwithsharonwatson.com/illuminating-literature-when-worlds-collide-gateway/ .

Suggested Teaching Schedule for a Book-of-the-Month Club

When I conduct a book-of-the-month club, our very first meeting includes fun icebreakers and a few minutes on how the club is going to work. Then I address literature and conflict. After our break, I set up the first book for them, talking about what to look for, who the author is, and any literary terms or writers' devices they should know ahead of time.

In subsequent meetings, I use the first and largest time slot (1 and ½ hours) to follow up on the book students have just read. We talk about its themes, issues, and so forth. After a short break, I use the next time slot (1 hour) to set up the next book so they know what to look for and are not going into the book cold.

The sections on the next page correspond to the headings and subheadings found in the student's textbook. In each month, students will need to bring the current novel and the next novel to class.

Month 1

Start Here (1 hour) Welcome • What Is Literature? • This Course's Philosophy • Bilbo Against . . . Well, Everyone • Two More Ways of Looking at Conflict • Evaluate! (if there's time, do this in class)

5-minute BREAK

Pudd'nhead Wilson: Set up (1 ½ hours) Suggested Reading and Homework Plan: Preview (explain the schedule and what is due at what times) • Imitate! (explain what it is and when it is due) • Text and Context • Conflicts • Literary Terms: Foreshadowing and Irony • Your Novel Notebook • Too Good to Forget •Setting and Year of Publication •Read "A Whisper to the Reader" • Your Choice of Activities (explain)

Anything not listed in the above schedule or not finished in class is left for students to complete at home.

Month 2

Pudd'nhead Wilson: Follow up (1 ½ hours) Five-Star Report • Colliding Worlds • Conflicts • The Curse of Ham • Your Novel Notebook • Questions for Discussion

5-minute BREAK with York Peppermint Patties (York is a character's name) as a reward.

The War of the Worlds: Set up (1 hour) Suggested Reading and Homework Plan: Preview (explain the schedule and what is due at what times) • Imitate! (explain what it is and when it is due or do in class in teams of two) • The Genre • Writers' Device: Reaction •Literary Terms: Alliteration and Allusion • Your Novel Notebook • Your Choice of Activities (explain)

Anything not listed in the above schedule or not finished in class is left for students to complete at home.

Month 3

The War of the Worlds: Follow up (1 ½ hours) Five-Star Report • Colliding Worlds • Conflicts • Writer's Device: Empathetic Character • Your Novel Notebook • Questions for Discussion • Your Choice of Activities ("Choose Your Invader" can be fun if done in class; create teams, assign methods of chronicling, and let students present their results after 30 minutes.)

5-minute BREAK with lollipops (Lick Observatory) as a reading reward.

The Friendly Persuasion: Set up (1 hour) This Is Different • Suggested Reading and Homework Plan: Preview (explain the schedule and what is due at what times) • Imitate! (explain or do this in class in teams of two) • Literary Terms: Simile and Metaphor • Your Novel Notebook • Literary Terms: Mood and Tone • Setting and

Publication Dates • The First Six Chapters (explain the assignment) • The Last Eight Chapters (explain the assignment) • Your Novel Notebook • Your Choice of Activities (explain what this is and when it is due)

Anything not listed in the above schedule or not finished in class is left for students to complete at home.

Month 4
The Friendly Persuasion: Follow up (1 ½ hours) Five-Star Report • Questions for Discussion 1 (for the first six chapters) • Questions for Discussion 2 (for the last eight chapters) • Except for Me and Thee • Your Novel Notebook Follow-up • Fun Fact Follow-up • The Double Meaning

5-minute BREAK with cookies of some sort to represent the rock cookies Mattie took to Gard's mother to welcome her to the neighborhood.

Peter Pan: Set up (1 hour) Suggested Reading and Homework Plan: Preview (explain the schedule and what is due at what times) • Imitate! (explain and give due date) • Meet Sir Barrie (explain that they will be researching and filling in blanks this month) • Literary Terms: Symbol and Motif • Writers' Devices: Tense and Prolepsis • NO ACTIVITIES THIS MONTH—YAY!

Anything not listed in the above schedule or not finished in class is left for students to complete at home.

Month 5
Peter Pan: Follow up (1 ½ hours) Meet Sir Barrie • Colliding Worlds • Writers' Devices: Apostrophe and Authorial Intrusion • Discussion Questions • Your Novel Notebook • The Hero's Journey (Do any students want to share their personal version of the hero's journey from their Novel Notebooks?)

5-minute BREAK with Milky Way bars as a reading reward.

Warriors Don't Cry: Set up (1 hour) Suggested Reading and Homework Plan: Preview (explain the schedule and what is due at what times) • Imitate! (explain and give due date) • A Memoir • Point of View and Voice • Appetizers • Your Novel Notebook (Tell them which questions you want them to answer, if you wish.) • Your Choice of Activities (explain when this is due)

Anything not listed in the above schedule or not finished in class is left for students to complete at home.

Month 6

Warriors Don't Cry: Follow up (1 ½ hours) Five-Star Report • Colliding Worlds • Melba and the Hero's Journey • Your Novel Notebook • Questions for Discussion • Anything else of your choice if there's time (Literary Terms: Analogy, Euphemism, and Hyperbole; student Activities, and so forth)

5-minute BREAK with Cadbury Eggs to represent the egg thrown on Melba.

A Tale of Two Cities: Set up (1 hour) Suggested Reading and Homework Plan: Preview (explain the schedule and what is due at what times) • Imitate! (class discussion on how Dickens achieves a gloomy, foreboding mood that telegraphs death and give due date or write this in class in teams of two) • Genre and Setting • Backstory • Literary Terms: Theme and Christ Figure (themes in general and this particular theme of death and resurrection) • Your Novel Notebook • Writers' Device: Setup and Payoff • Stuff You Might Want to Know + Chapter Questions (Explain that this section will be super helpful to have handy as they read the story; in addition, tell them which questions you want them to answer along the way, if you wish.)

Anything not listed in the above schedule or not finished in class is left for students to complete at home.

Month 7

A Tale of Two Cities: Follow up (1 ½ hours) Five-Star Report • Colliding Worlds • Vocabulary Quizzola (review) • Send the Manuscript Back! (discussion) • A Motif • Your Novel Notebook • Questions for Discussion

5-minute BREAK with any candies in small cartons to signify Sydney Carton's sacrifice.

Fahrenheit 451: Set up (1 hour) Suggested Reading and Homework Plan: Preview (explain the schedule and what is due at what times) • Imitate! (give a due date) • Genre • The Man's Got Style • Publication Date and Setting • Your Novel Notebook • A Warning

Anything not listed in the above schedule or not finished in class is left for students to complete at home.

Month 8

Fahrenheit 451: Follow up (1 ½ hours) Five-Star Report • Colliding Worlds • NO VOCABULARY QUIZZOLA THIS MONTH • Literary Element: Plot • Up or Down? • Motifs Again • Allusions to Christian Stories or Phrases • Writers' Device: The Telling Detail • A Dark and Sinister Warning • Your Novel Notebook (How did their technology-free experiment turn out?) • Questions for Discussion

5-minute BREAK with Twizzlers (strawberry) to tie in with Clarisse, or Red Hots to tie in with fire and burning, or some s'more-flavored candy.

The Screwtape Letters: Set up (1 hour) Suggested Reading and Homework Plan: Preview (explain the schedule and what is due at what times) • Imitate! (give a due date) • Literary License • Literary Terms: Epistolary Novel and Satire • Writer's Device: Connotations • Front Matter and a Heads Up • Your Novel Notebook (Tell students which questions you want them to answer, if you wish.)

Anything not listed in the above schedule or not finished in class is left for students to complete at home.

Month 9
The Screwtape Letters: Follow up and end-of-year party (1 ½ - 2 hours) Five-Star Report • Colliding Worlds • Your Novel Notebook • Questions for Discussion • Celebratory party with devil's food cake or cupcakes

ANSWER KEY AND GUIDE

Chapter 0: Start Here

Teacher, this chapter is an introduction to literature and this year's theme of conflict, When Worlds Collide. Students will begin reading *Pudd'nhead Wilson* in the next chapter.

The bold-face headings you see below coordinate with the headings in the student textbook. This is true throughout this guide, with the exception of Facebook Posts and Objectives.

Objectives

Objectives for this chapter are as follows (Revise or add to this list, as desired):

- To introduce the topic of literature in a nonthreatening manner.
- To help students understand the terms *literature* and *literary classics*.
- To encourage students to think about why people read literature.
- To encourage students to think about what they want to learn in this course.
- To discuss questions about literature.
- To learn the literary terms *conflict, antagonist,* and *protagonist*.
- To understand the kinds of conflict present in any well-written story by reviewing each conflict in the light of the character Bilbo Baggins from J. R. R. Tolkien's *The Hobbit*.
- To look at conflict from the writer's perspective.
- To evaluate a story of the student's choice based on its conflicts and to draw conclusions about which conflict is most important to that story.

Lesson 1

Welcome!

Which books in this year's list do you think will be your favorites? If you have already read some of them, what did you think of them? *Let students weigh in on these questions and let them express their ideas of the books.*

What Is Literature?

The terms *literary classics* or *the classics* refer to stories, poems, and plays that have not been written recently but have stood the test of time. In your opinion, what book written recently will be a literary classic in fifty years? Write your answer below: *Answers will vary.*

Why are older books so boring? (Substitute your own word for *boring* such as *dull* or *slow*, if desired.) *A suggested list of reasons appears on pages 3-4 of the textbook.*

Students are to add their own reason why they or other readers may find older books dull or difficult to read.

Why should I read and study literature anyway? Isn't it good enough that I read lots of popular novels, sci-fi, historical romance, and so forth, on my own? *Students have a variety of boxes to check on pages 4-5. In addition, students will add one reason to study literature.*

What do I want to learn from this course? *Students have a variety of boxes to check on pages 5-6. In addition, students will add one item to the list.*

Grades

Students are learning what they will be graded on. See your generic Grading Grid on page 3 of this guide. Find specific ones at the end of each chapter.

Your Novel Notebook

Students are learning that they need to obtain and use an extra notebook for this course.

For a FREE download of a colorful Novel Notebook with all the questions already in it, go to http://writingwithsharonwatson.com/illuminating-literature-when-worlds-collide-gateway/.

This Course's Philosophy

This course's philosophy is that these books are written by flawed humans who struggled with—or gave in to—sin and their sin natures, who may or may not have been Christians, whose stories may or may not agree with the truths written in the Bible, but whose stories reflect some redeeming truth and are, therefore, worth reading.

While literature can be uplifting and spur us to greatness, it also can be a disturbing reflection of our fallen state.

Teacher, these questions are suggested in this section in the student textbook: Why do some people have such an emotional attachment to classics? Why do they have an emotional attachment to any book or movie? *Possible reasons appear on page 7. You may want to tell a story about a book of literature that is meaningful to you.*

Lesson 2

Colliding Worlds?

Teacher, these questions are suggested in this section and can be used for discussion, if you wish:

What conflicts did the pigs experience in "The Three Little Pigs"? *Against another character (the wolf's threats and his huffing and puffing), against nature (the building materials), and against themselves (Can they come up with a solution each time they are threatened?)*

What do you think a female hero should be called? *Student opinion*

Students are also learning the terms **protagonist** and **antagonist**.
Conflicts:
1. The character against himself or herself
2. The character against another character
3. The character against society
4. The character against nature
5. The character against God/the gods/fate
6. The character against technology/biotechnology

Bilbo Against . . . Well, Everyone

Teacher, these conflicts ("the character against . . .") are fleshed out in the textbook in the life of Bilbo Baggins from J. R. R. Tolkien's *The Hobbit*. Each conflict in the list is explained with examples from Bilbo's life.

Two More Ways of Looking at Conflict

A second way of looking at conflict in a literature class is to categorize the forces of antagonism like this:

- ✓ *Internal* (doubts, fears, moral laziness, being a loner, and things of that nature)
- ✓ *External* (a gossiping friend, a system of harmful rules, or an attack of vampire zombies).

A third way of examining conflict is taught in fiction-writing classes:

- ✓ What are the lead's (main character's) **goals** and who or what is keeping him from them? For instance, if his goal is to find the buried treasure, characters from the story and other forces of antagonism are going to try to keep him from getting it.
- ✓ What is the lead's **deep desire**? For example, is he seeking this buried treasure because his dad is a famous treasure hunter and he wants to earn

his father's respect? Does he know he has this deep yearning? How is he sabotaging himself concerning this desire?

Lesson 3

Evaluate!

Every novel, short story, play, TV show, movie, and comic book has a conflict. Even most songs contain conflicts: "I love him, but he doesn't even know I exist," for example. Think of a story you have read or a movie you've seen lately and evaluate the main character's conflicts. Then list them under the appropriate headings below.

Note: Not every story will contain all the conflicts. *Students have room in the textbook on pages 15-17 to write their answers after each category. Answers will vary based on the book selected.*

Title of book or story:_____
1. The character against himself or herself
2. The character against another character
3. The character against society
4. The character against nature
5. The character against God/the gods/fate
6. The character against technology/biotechnology

In your opinion, which one of the above types of conflict is the strongest or the most important conflict in the story you chose? Answer in the space below and then answer the next two questions: *Answers will vary according to the selected book.*

What is the lead's main goal? *Answers will vary.*
What is the lead's deep desire? *Answers will vary.*

Teacher, you may want to use this exercise as a discussion starter by asking students to report what they found or to make sure they understand the material.

Chapter 1: *Pudd'nhead Wilson*

Dover Publications   ISBN: 0-486-40885-X

Facebook Posts

If your group or co-op meets monthly, you may want to keep in touch with the students and keep them interested in the novels by creating a secret Facebook group for them and their parents. Below are the questions I've asked my Facebook group. Feel free to devise your own questions or find your own links to interesting material.

- What is the absolutely worst fiction book you've ever read? Tell us why it was so awful.
- Talk about irony . . . Mark Twain never liked his daughter Clara's choice of husband, and the two men never got along. But guess where both men are buried. Yes, they are buried in the family plot in Elmira, New York. But it gets worse than that. Clara had a monument erected that is two fathoms tall (the "mark twain" of Sam Clemens' steamboat days). It features two medallions, each with a profile of the two most important men in her life: her dad and her husband—two men who disliked each other but are memorialized together forever on the monument.

  What is ironic in your life? Or what have you seen in your friends' lives or in the world in general that is ironic?
- What is one of your favorite books?
- Pudd'nhead (David) Wilson is from Upstate New York. Why do you think Twain uses a Northern character to be in a book about a Southern issue?
- Here's a link to a short, short bio of Mark Twain on YouTube: https://www.youtube.com/watch?v=vuQMBWjmlHk. Watch it and tell us what you think.
- If you could sit down with Mark Twain (or Samuel Clemens) today, what would you ask him?
- Tom Driscoll (Roxy's real son Chambers) was raised with every advantage, yet his character, which Roxy attributed to his drop of black blood, kept tripping him up. Is a person's life determined by how he is raised or by what he is born with?
- Mark Twain enjoyed keeping scrapbooks filled with souvenirs, reviews of his books, photographs, and so forth. He even invented a self-pasting scrapbook that actually made him some money. You can read about his scrapbook patent here: https://docs.google.com/viewer?url=patentimages.storage.googleapis.com/pdfs/US140245.pdf . If you were to keep a scrapbook of your life, what would you put in it? You can be as general or specific as you like.

Before You Read the Book

Teacher, you may want to plan on distributing a small reward to students who complete reading *Pudd'nhead Wilson*. Let the reward refer to something in the book, and let students guess what it refers to. For example, you can distribute black and white pencils, black licorice, some candy that is available in milk and white chocolate, York Peppermint Patties, or boxes of Good & Plenty to highlight the theme of prejudice based on skin color. I'm always surprised to learn how much the students look forward to this small reward and how much they enjoy figuring out the sometimes silly tie-in to the novel, no matter how big a groaner the tie-in is!

Lesson 1

Suggested Reading and Homework Plan: Preview

Teacher, below is the schedule your students are following. Please let them know if you expect them to use another schedule and tell them when the activity is due.

Week 1:
- ❑ Complete lessons 1-4.

Week 2:
- ❑ Read chapters I – XII of *Pudd'nhead Wilson*.

Week 3:
- ❑ Read chapters XIII – XXI of *Pudd'nhead Wilson*.

Week 4:
- ❑ Decide on one activity and begin work on it. You'll find the list of activities at the end of this chapter. **Your teacher will tell you when this is due.**
- ❑ Complete lessons 5-7.
- ❑ Hand in your activity and breathe a sigh of relief.

Imitate!

As an example of something written well, turn to the chapter "The Nymph Revealed" and read the paragraph on page 47 that begins like this: "A gigantic eruption, like that of Krakatoa a few years ago, ..." The paragraph is comparing a life-altering revelation and its effects on Tom to a huge volcanic explosion and eruption.

Most likely, you have had something cataclysmic happen to you, too, or you have watched a friend go through something catastrophic.

Choose a natural disaster and then write about your own personal upheaval or that of your friend's. Use verbs and word images normally associated with the natural disaster.

Teacher: If you have time in class, you may want to use this as an in-class writing opportunity so students can learn by what their peers have written. If you are teaching a co-op, the paragraph can be due in a week or emailed to you.

Lesson 2

Text and Context

Objectives:
- To learn the terms *text* and *context* as they apply to reading novels.
- To understand how a novel's context can affect the novel's interpretation and meaning.

Teacher, students are learning about text and context. The novel or short story is the primary source or what is called the **text**.

The **context** is all the stuff outside the story that may color it and put it in a different light: the author's upbringing; events that were shaping the author and the world at the time; the moral, spiritual, or ethical temperature of those first readers; and so forth. In the figure below, the story is the *text*, and the squares are the *context* through which it is viewed or interpreted.

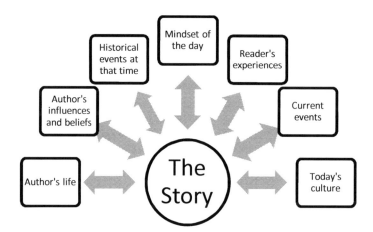

Christian readers will read the text and want to understand the context, but they also will want to evaluate everything they read through the filter of the truths in the Bible. It will look something like this to those readers. This is a simplification of the process and result, but you get the idea:

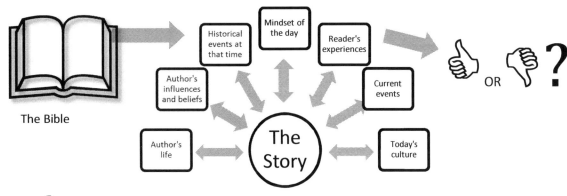

Lesson 3

Meet Mr. Twain . . . or Is it Mr. Clemens?

Objective: To get to know Mark Twain better and to discover how much of his life experiences and beliefs influence *Pudd'nhead Wilson.*

Teacher, students are reading about Twain and the duality of his life, which will be reflected in *Pudd'nhead Wilson.*

Write two things about his life that you find interesting: *Answers will vary.*

Lesson 4

Conflicts

Students are filling in the list of conflicts as a means of review.

1. Character against *himself or herself*
2. Character against *another character*
3. Character against *society*
4. Character against *nature*
5. Character against *God/the gods/fate*
6. Character against *technology/biotechnology*

Pseudonym

If you wrote with a pseudonym, what one would you choose? Why would you choose that one? *Answers will vary.*

Fun Fact

Students are learning Twain's fascination with twins and pairs of people. One such story he wrote is *Those Extraordinary Twins,* which used to be part of *Pudd'nhead Wilson* before Twain expunged it from the story. Students can read or hear *Those Extraordinary Twins* at http://www.gutenberg.org.

Read Twain's fascinating Author's Note to *Those Extraordinary Twins* at http://www.classicbookshelf.com/library/mark_twain/ the_tragedy_of_pudd_nhead_wilson/23/.

Literary Terms: Foreshadowing and Irony

Objective: To learn the literary terms *foreshadowing* and *irony* so students can look for them in the story.

Teacher, students are learning the terms foreshadowing and irony.

Your Novel Notebook

Objectives:
- To identify instances of foreshadowing, irony, and prejudice.
- To practice reading with intent to glean insight.

Teacher, below is the list of items your students will be compiling in their Novel Notebooks. You may want to discuss these with your students during the after-book discussion or simply ask to see their notebooks to make sure they compiled the lists. Adjust this list to your needs.

To download a FREE Novel Notebook with the questions already in it, go to http://writingwithsharonwatson.com/illuminating-literature-when-worlds-collide-gateway/ .

Answers to these questions appear in the section Questions for Discussion after the book is read.

1. Any of Mr. Wilson's witty sayings that you especially like.
2. Two examples of prejudice.
3. At least one place where Mark Twain uses foreshadowing.
4. Something ironic.
5. Any ideas about why *The Tragedy of Pudd'nhead Wilson* is, well, a tragedy for Pudd'nhead Wilson.

Too Good to Forget

Objective:
- To copy passages they like or don't like so they can learn from them.
- To learn to write well by imitating effective writing.

Setting and Year of Publication

Dawson's Landing was about fifty years old in 1830, and it was a growing river town in a slave state.

Year of publication: *1894.*

Are there any people or people groups in the United States or in the world today who are not considered human? *A few possibilities might be Jews in some countries, unborn babies, Christians being persecuted, children or adults with birth defects, and so on.*

Read "A Whisper to the Reader"

The first long sentence contains 179 words; the second contains 141. The name of the man William Hicks is boarding with in Italy is Macaroni Vermicelli, a name made up of two pastas.

Stuff You Might Want to Know

This section contains a dialect dictionary to define some of the words Twain uses. It also contains helpful bits of information to make the reading easier to understand. You may want to be aware that the word "nigger" is used often, presumably in the manner it was used historically.

Suggested Reading and Homework Plan

Week 1:
- ❑ Complete lessons 1-4. If you've been working along, you are through with the tasks for Week 1. If not, please complete them now.

Week 2:
- ❑ Read chapters I – XII of *Pudd'nhead Wilson*.

Week 3:
- ❑ Read chapters XIII – XXI of *Pudd'nhead Wilson*.

Week 4:
- ❑ Decide on one activity and begin work on it. You'll find the list of activities at the end of this chapter. **Your teacher will tell you when this is due.**
- ❑ Complete lessons 5-7.
- ❑ Hand in your activity and breathe a sigh of relief.

After You've Read the Book

Lesson 5

Five-Star Report

Teacher, students are filling out a grid to rate *Pudd'nhead Wilson* based on how they feel about the story. They are using this scale: 1 is "Couldn't stand it" and 5 is "Loved it."

Reward: Distribute a small reward to each student who finished reading *Pudd'nhead Wilson*, like a candy with both milk and white chocolate to tie in to the racial theme of black and white. I use York Peppermint Patties to allude to the black/white issues in this book and also because the judge who is the stepfather to Tom is York Driscoll. It's a real groaner, but the teens have fun guessing the tie-in.

Complete the Online Quizzes and Survey

Objectives:
- To complete a fact quiz online for a grade.
- To reinforce the terms they've learned so far in this text: conflict types, protagonist, antagonist, text, context, foreshadowing, irony, and pseudonym.
- To complete questions online to express opinions, interpret events in *Pudd'nhead Wilson,* and ponder what they would do in similar circumstances

Teacher, students are instructed to go to this address to get links to complete the following quizzes: http://WritingWithSharonWatson.com/illuminating-literature-when-worlds-collide-gateway/ .
- "Yes, I read it" Quiz—graded online for you
- Literary Terms Quiz (the list of 6 character conflicts + protagonist, antagonist, text, context, foreshadowing, irony, and pseudonym)—graded online for you
- Opinion Survey—no grade, but answers to the opinion questions may help you develop a strategy for your discussion time.

THESE ARE FREE QUIZZES. Students are allowed two attempts for the quizzes and one for the opinion survey. Also, the quiz site will email a full report of the quiz (questions, your student's answers, the correct answers, and your student's grade) to the email address your student signed in with.

Password for all online quizzes and the survey for *Pudd'nhead Wilson*: TWAIN.

If you prefer that students take the test without going online, use *Illuminating Literature: When Worlds Collide, Quiz and Answer Manual,* available for sale at http://writingwithsharonwatson.com/illuminating-literature-when-worlds-collide.

Opinion questions have no correct answer; students are graded on participation. Their answers to the opinion questions may help you develop a strategy for your discussion time.

Vocabulary Quizzola for *Pudd'nhead Wilson*

Objectives:
- To reinforce good vocabulary habits and awareness.
- To gain a grade, which is separate from the Grading Grid.

Directions: Match the definition on the right with the correct word on the left by entering the letter in the correct blank. The numbers after the words indicate page numbers where the words can be found in the Dover Thrift Edition of *Pudd'nhead Wilson*. **Ask your teacher if this is an open-book quiz.**

M___1. Indolent, 22	A. a mark of disgrace
K___2. Usurpation, 16	B. deep in thought
F___3. Sycophancy, 41	C. to scout out
E___4. Gibe, 81	D. property
D___5. Chattel, 47	E. to taunt; a taunt
A___6. Stigma, 84	F. flattery in order to gain something
O___7. Calaboose, 66	G. a mongrel dog (insulting to be called this)
L___8. Perdition, 57	H. apparent, but usually fake
P___9. Atrophied, 100	I. one who talks sheer nonsense
R___10. Grenadier, 40	J. generosity
I___11. Blatherskite, 42	K. taking someone else's place
N___12. Skiff, 61	L. a state of being lost; hell
T___13. Benefactor, 101	M. lazy
S___14. Teetotaler, 57	N. a small rowboat or sailboat
J___15. Magnanimity, 55	O. slang for *jail*
B___16. Pensive, 68	P. wasted away, not strong
H___17. Ostensible, 47	Q. done by stealth, sneaky
C___18. Reconnoiter, 49	R. a soldier
Q___19. Surreptitious, 51	S. one who abstains from alcoholic drinks
G___20. Cur, 62	T. one who does good for others

Total number correct_____
Vertical word encoded in your correct answers: *PRINTS*
Teacher, each correct answer is worth 5 points.

Lesson 6

Colliding Worlds

Teacher, below are some suggestions. Your student may think of other worlds that are colliding in *Pudd'nhead Wilson*.
1. *Slave vs. Free*
2. *Slavery vs. Freedom*
3. *Black vs. White*
4. *Poor vs. Rich*
5. *Wise vs. Foolish*
6. *Industry vs. Laziness*
7. *Science vs. Narrow-mindedness*
8. *Honor vs. Dishonor*
9. *Expectation vs. Reality*

- What happens when these worlds collide? *There are a few answers in the textbook, but students will think of others.*
- Choose one conflict from *Pudd'nhead Wilson*. In your opinion, how could it have been prevented? Write your answer below: *Answers will vary.*
- If you were on a fact-finding mission and found *Pudd'nhead Wilson* in the corner of some dilapidated brick building, what would you surmise about their culture? What wisdom would you bring back to make life better today? Write your answer below: *(This question is based on Job 8:8-9 "Ask the former generations and find out what their fathers learned, for we were born only yesterday and know nothing, and our days on earth are but a shadow.") Answers will vary.*

Conflicts

Teacher, below are some possibilities for the conflict lists for Pudd'nhead Wilson, Roxy, and Tom (the real Chambers).

Pudd'nhead Wilson
1. Pudd'nhead Wilson vs. himself: *He begins to doubt the existence of the knife and, therefore, his plan to catch its thief.*
2. Pudd'nhead Wilson vs. another character: *At the trial, he is working against the true murderer, Tom Driscoll (the real Valet de Chambre or "Chambers").*
3. Pudd'nhead Wilson vs. society: *His joke about the dog falls on humorless ears, and the town brands him as stupid for years. He is unable to practice law in that town because of their small-mindedness.*
4. Pudd'nhead Wilson vs. nature: *He struggles for days trying to find a match for the fingerprint on the knife, using his extensive collection of villagers' prints.*
5. Pudd'nhead Wilson vs. God/the gods/fate: *He belongs to the Society of Free-thinkers, a common type of society in that era for talking about and believing in ideas that often ran contrary to those in the Bible. Religion is viewed negatively, and logic, facts, and science in a positive light. The two, religion and science, are viewed as mutually exclusive. But it doesn't show up as a conflict in this book.*

Roxy
1. Roxy vs. herself: *She thinks about suicide and is an enemy to herself the way she fawns on the new Tom Driscoll and helps to spoil him.*
2. Roxy vs. another character: *Percy Driscoll when he accuses the slaves of thievery and almost sells Roxy; Tom Driscoll as he often treats her cruelly and finally sells her down the river. She fears Pudd'nhead Wilson would see through her deception with the babies.*
3. Roxy vs. society: *The whole idea that she is considered black and therefore a slave even though she looks white and is only one-sixteenth black. The fact that she is a slave at all pits society against her.*
4. Roxy vs. nature: *Develops arthritis in her arms and is no longer able to work on the steamboats to support herself.*

5. Roxy vs. God/the gods/fate: *A statement she makes on page 11 about God, and from her point of view, it is a good question: "God was good to you [the original Tom Driscoll]; why warn't he good to him [her slave child]?" She blames God for the meanness of men.*

Tom Driscoll (the real Chambers)
1. Tom vs. himself: *a gambler, a spoiled rich boy who lords it over everyone. Fights briefly—very briefly—with himself about selling his own mother down the river. Hard hearted (p. 95). Kills his adoptive uncle for money. He is his own worst enemy.*
2. Tom vs. another character: *The man to whom he owes money gives him trouble. Roxy threatens to tell who he really is if he doesn't straighten up. He is constantly at odds with his uncle over behavior, money, and the will.*
3. Tom vs. society: *The secret workings of the silent fingerprints threaten his life and promise to throw him into a black world of slavery. He is finally made a slave and sold down the river.*
4. Tom vs. nature: *His own fingerprints are against him. He struggles with himself and his behavior but blames his "black" blood for it.*
5. Tom vs. God/the gods/fate: *No overt struggle with God from Tom's point of view except that he believes the "curse of Ham" is upon him. He does struggle with his idea of fate as seen through his "one drop" of black blood. Is he destined to be a failure because of this? He wrestles with this briefly. From the reader's point of view, we see him constantly choose the wrong path when he has the opportunity to choose the right one.*

Which character in *Pudd'nhead Wilson* has the strongest goals, is working the hardest toward them, and has the most plans to achieve them? Which character has the deepest desires, the most heart-felt yearnings, and moves those yearnings from internal to external by doing something about them? Which one has the strongest forces of antagonism against him or her because of those goals or desires?

This character is the true protagonist of *Pudd'nhead Wilson*. Write the name of the character below: *Roxy*

The Curse of Ham

Objective: To straighten out incorrect thinking about the curse of Ham, its origins, and its implications.

On page 47 of *Pudd'nhead Wilson*, you will find this sentence: "He said to himself that the curse of Ham was upon him." Who is saying this to himself? Write your answer here: *Tom Driscoll (the real Chambers)*
  • Who was Ham? *Noah's youngest son*
  • Whom did Noah curse? *Canaan, a son of Ham*

- What was the curse? *That Canaan would be a slave to his brothers, which was fulfilled in part when the "ites" of the land of Canaan became the slaves of the Israelites.*

Lesson 7

Questions for Discussion

Objectives:
- To give students a chance to ask the teacher questions about the book.
- To give students a chance to discuss important topics brought up by the book such as slavery, fate, nurture versus nature, adoption, suicide, and so forth.

Teacher, there is no way you can discuss all these questions with your students. Choose the questions that are appropriate to your class and the topics you want to discuss. Some of the answers are labeled "Answers will vary" or "Student opinion." While some of the answers to these discussion questions really are "Student opinion," you can guide the discussion and facilitate a better understanding of godly thinking and actions through many of these questions, especially when they have moral or ethical implications.

These questions are for discussion *or* for writing assignments. Feel free to choose the ones you feel will be most helpful to your teens. In addition, after reading the responses your teens entered in *Pudd'nhead Wilson* Opinion Survey, you might want to adjust your discussion time according to what you find there.

To get the discussion time going, ask students these questions:

1. What questions do you have about *Pudd'nhead Wilson*?
2. What aspects of this book appealed to you?
3. What is your impression of this book?

These preliminary questions will help to clear up any misunderstandings or miscomprehensions from the book, and they'll get students talking during the discussion session because they are open-ended questions. Students can answer other students' questions, too. This pre-discussion time may also serve to answer some of the questions printed below or can be a springboard to any of the aspects of the book you want to focus on.

The first five questions are not really questions but the lists students were compiling in their Novel Notebooks.

1. Any of Mr. Wilson's witty sayings that you especially like. *Answers will vary.*
2. Two examples of prejudice. *Prejudice against David Wilson who is from the North and who tells jokes the locals can't understand; Roxy's ironic prejudice*

against Jasper, who is darker than she; prejudice for the twins at first because they are so likeable and such a novelty and then against the twins for being foreigners from Italy; prejudice against slaves; prejudice against blacks; prejudice against anyone with "one drop" of black blood in them; Tom's prejudice against Pudd'nhead because Tom believes him to be an idiot who couldn't possibly figure out the truth; Tom's prejudice against Judge Driscoll for having money when Tom doesn't; Judge Driscoll's prejudice against anyone who doesn't have what he perceives as "honor"; and so forth.

3. At least one place where Mark Twain uses foreshadowing. *The fact that Roxy switched the boys with each other promises trouble ahead. The introduction of the fingerprint hobby and the twins' knife (55) are clever use of the foreshadowing device. Roxy declares that she can tell the two boys apart but Percy (the father of one of them) can't. Tom's gambling: "It would not do to gamble where his uncle could hear of it; he knew that quite well" (23). If someone has a vice in the beginning of the story, it should get him into trouble later (and it does). Of Tom: "He was getting into deep waters. He was taking chances, privately, which might get him into trouble some day—in fact,* did*" (23). Tom: "'I've struck bottom this time; there's nothing lower.' But that was a hasty conclusion" (41). When Pudd'nhead picks up Tom's hand to read the palm, he sees something, and Tom pulls his hand away (56). The judge's prophecy about the knife and an assassination (90).*

4. Something ironic. *Students have many options with this because there's plenty of irony in this story! Roxy appears white but is considered black, which is accentuated in reverse when Wilson hears her speak outside his window and assumes she is black. It is ironic that Roxy considers Jasper too dark for her, even though the town would consider them as equals. Wilson is intelligent but is considered a dunce by townsfolk who are the real dunces. It's ironic that Wilson belongs to a society that call themselves "Free-thinkers," yet they do not think freely about the slave issue but believe the culture's values on slavery and blacks. Tom, a "white" in disguise and who as Roxy says is only "imitation white," chooses yet another disguise when he steals (dressing as a young woman and an old black woman). Verbal irony when Tom says, "A man's own hand is his deadliest enemy!" (54) when referring to palm reading; his hand does become his deadliest enemy when he uses it to kill the judge. The Judge's verbal irony occurs when he says, "Do you mean to tell me that blood of my race" went to court instead of challenging Luigi to a duel (62); also, it is ironic when he declares, "A coward in my family! A Driscoll a coward!" (63) because Tom is not in his family and is not a Driscoll. It's ironic that when the Judge sets up the duel with Luigi, he calls the twin "a darling" and means it, even though he is an enemy in this duel (71). Tom says his uncle is going to "patch up the family honor" (74), knowing full well he does not belong to the judge's family. It's ironic that Roxy gets some of her chutzpah and regality from her belief that the white people Captain Smith and Pocahontas are in her lineage instead of getting it from her black ancestry (76). Tom hates Luigi "for kicking him" (80) but then turns right around and "kicks" the local constable ("You have a good*

reputation—for a country detective") and Wilson, jabbing them in their most tender spots while appearing innocent of hurtful speech; Twain couches the verbal attack in physical terms: "The constable hadn't anything handy to hit back with" (82). It's ironic that Roxy is transported to her life of slavery downriver in a steamboat, the same kind she'd worked on as a free woman (88). It's ironic that Tom thinks his mother is "dead to all motherly instincts" (95) when he is in trouble because, really, motherliness has been at the heart of Roxy the whole story and she's already sacrificed her freedom to get him out of trouble. Perhaps the final irony is that Tom (the real Chambers) is pardoned from the murder so he can be sold to pay for the debts of a man who died eight years ago, as Tom had not been listed on the original inventory of the estate (122). The title is ironic: Pudd'nhead ends up better off in the end of the story, and most of the other characters end up tragically worse off.

5. Any ideas about why Mark Twain's original title for this book is *The Tragedy of Pudd'nhead Wilson. Answers will vary. Try this one on for size: Even though he is from the North and knows who killed the judge, he is unable (or unwilling) to effect a change in society. His knowledge only breaks people; it does not help them.*

Questions to get the facts straight:

6. How does Tom Driscoll's father differentiate the babies from one another? *By the difference in their clothing (12-13).*

7. What happens on September 4 to scare Roxy into changing the babies around? *Percy Driscoll sold most of his slaves because he suspected them of thievery. Roxy didn't want to be sold or separated from her son through a slave sale. (8-9)*

8. Who is the biological father of Roxy's child? *Colonel Cecil Burleigh Essex, a First Family of Virginia member, white and now dead (3, 44).*

9. Who is the girl Pudd'nhead Wilson saw in Tom's bedroom? *Tom dressing as a girl so he could steal things and not get caught (49).*

10. How does Tom pay his gambling debts? *By stealing (49) and by selling his mother into slavery (87-88).*

Questions on the topics of abortion and suicide:

1. When Sam Clemens was a young reporter in San Francisco, he lost his job, was broke, and then put in jail for drunkenness. Shortly afterward, he put a gun to his head and almost pulled the trigger. Unbeknownst to him, his newest short story was a wild hit back East. In *Pudd'nhead Wilson*, Roxy almost commits suicide three times. What could you tell Sam or Roxy to convince either of them not to commit suicide? *Answers will vary. Lead the students to understand that events, situations, and circumstances change. What may be true today might not be true for a person tomorrow. Help them*

understand they have a reason for being on this earth, that they are precious, and that they will not always be this sad, lonely, or negative about themselves.

2. In "Roxy Plays a Shrewd Trick," Roxy is in terror of her infant son growing up and being sold down the river, so she declares to him that she has "to kill you to save you, honey." Compare her statement with this question some abortion counselors ask their clients: "Can you see abortion as a 'loving act' toward your children and yourself?"[1] *Lead students to understand that abortion is not a "loving act" toward the baby, despite the circumstances of the mother, especially as there are other alternatives such as adoption available to today's unwilling mothers. Help them see that killing a child is not saving it. You may want to discuss abortion procedures, pain to the baby during abortion, or other topics to help them understand the negative nature of abortion and infanticide. Guide students to understand that both slavery and abortion/infanticide break the most precious mother-child bond by tearing them apart. None is a "loving act." None will "save" the child.*

Questions on the topic of how we view ourselves and others:

1. *Why is Roxy treated so poorly at the plantation? The plain-looking wife of the plantation owner is envious of Roxy's good looks, so she makes her a field slave instead of a house slave. This question also ties in to the topic of prejudice because the plantation owner's wife was envious of Roxy and so treated her with prejudice.*

2. The electioneering in "The Judge Utters Dire Prophecy" is conducted with bribery, innuendo, scoffing, derision, lies, using facts out of context, impugning the twins' characters and leveling ridicule against them. Facts were not used properly. Give an example from everyday life when people use any of the negative strategies listed above to harm someone or to sway others. *Student opinion*

3. Apply the following quotations to any of the characters in *Pudd'nhead Wilson* or to something that happened to you. The second quotation is spoken by Schmendrick, a magician who is still learning his trade and is viewed as a bungler. He is speaking to a caged unicorn. *Answers will vary.*

   i. The eyes of others our prisons; their thoughts our cages. (Virginia Woolf)

   ii. "It's a rare man who is taken for what he truly is," [Schmendrick] said.   "There is much misjudgment in the world. Now I knew you for a unicorn when I first saw you, and I know that I am your friend. Yet you take me for a clown, or a clod, or a betrayer, and so must I be if you see me so. The magic on you is only magic and will vanish as soon as you are free, but the enchantment of error that you put on me I must wear forever in your eyes." (*The Last Unicorn* by Peter S. Beagle)

4. When Judge Driscoll hears from a friend that Tom didn't challenge Luigi to a duel, the judge faints. At home, he yells at Tom and calls him a coward. Later, Tom lies and explains that he didn't challenge Luigi to a duel because he thought it would be dishonorable to challenge an admitted killer to a duel, to which Judge Driscoll agrees. This "massaging the story" happens all the time in news reports and in real life. How is it that *when* you hear a story and *how* you hear it affects your perception of it? *Answers will vary.*

5. If you can't tell a person's race by the color of his or her skin, what does race matter? Is outer appearance an artificial line? *Answers will vary. Though different people groups enjoy varying cultures, the biblical view of man is that we are all one race descended from Adam and then from Noah.*

6. What role does fate play in our lives? What role does ancestry play? What role does environment play? What role does personal choice play? *Answers will vary.*

7. Tom Driscoll (Roxy's real son Chambers) was raised with every advantage, yet his character, which Roxy attributed to his drop of black blood, kept tripping him up. Is a person's life determined by how he is raised or by what he is born with? *Answers will vary.*

8. What are ways that people can sell each other downriver? In what ways do you sell someone downriver, metaphorically speaking? *Answers will vary.*

9. Have you ever felt out of place somewhere? When is this a good thing? When is it a bad thing? *It's a good thing to feel out of place when people are asking you to do things you know or suspect are wrong, as in I Peter 4:4. Students' answers will vary when it comes to a bad thing to feel out of place.*

10. Who or what do you want to be? How much of it is what you've been born with or been given? How much is what you do to make it happen? *Answers will vary. Hopefully, students will realize they can make a change and overcome negative aspects of their characters, personalities, bodies (handicaps or perceived ugliness), and family situations.*

If You Liked This Book

Students are viewing a list of books similar to *Pudd'nhead Wilson* in theme or black/white topics.

Can't Get Enough of Mark Twain?

For more information on Mark Twain, try these Web sites:
- http://www.marktwainmuseum.org
- http://www.elmira.edu/academics/Academic_Resources/Library/Collections/Mark_Twain_Archive.html
- http://www.pbs.org/marktwain
- http://www.marktwaincountry.com/mark-twain

The first one will give you information about his life in Hannibal, Missouri, including pictures of his old house and how he developed some of his characters from people he knew. The second one will give you information of his adult life and his summers at the Quarry Farm on the outskirts of Elmira, New York, where he wrote much of *The Adventures of Tom Sawyer* and other famous books.

This is the end of lesson 7.

Your Choice of Activities

Objectives:
- To choose and complete one activity and share the results with the class, group, or interested party.
- To be an active, not passive, participant in the world of the book.

Choose only one of the following activities. Read all of them carefully before you make your decision. Below you will find a short explanation of each activity. **Your teacher will tell you when this is due.**

- A Calendar—Create witty sayings for your own calendar.
- The Artist in You—Paint or draw a scene or character from the book.
- Find Your Roots—Research your genealogy.
- With a Friend—Interview someone of a different ethnic background than yours.
- I'll Watch the Movie—Compare book to movie and give a movie review.
- You're the Expert—Research and write a short essay on fingerprinting, twins, conjoined twins, or blood.
- Sometimes I Feel like a Motherless Child—Explore the musical world of spirituals.
- Double the Trouble—Write a short story about twins or other topic of interest.
- Unrelated—Write a short story using five unrelated props and a twist.
- Black Is Beautiful—Investigate famous African Americans or international blacks.
- History Buff—Create a timeline of major events in African American or black history or research another topic concerning race, racism, modern slavery, and so forth.

A Calendar

The calendar in *Pudd'nhead Wilson* was similar to Benjamin Franklin's *Poor Richard's Almanac* into which Franklin inserted plenty of original quips and sayings. Even today many people like to buy a tear-off calendar that includes a word of the day, a comic strip, or a witty saying for each day.

Design your own calendar. Include pictures and plenty of aphorisms.

The Artist in You

The Mark Twain Boyhood Home & Museum in Hannibal, Missouri, boasts a fascinating model for a projected sculpture that never was completed. It is comprised of characters from four of Twain's books, standing or sitting, artfully arranged. Draw or paint your own picture of an exciting event or person in *Pudd'nhead Wilson*. Include a caption for your picture. Or create a diorama (a creative miniaturization) of a critical scene or sculpt something or someone from the book.

Find Your Roots

The famous black poet Langston Hughes writes this in his memoir:

> "You see, unfortunately, I am not black. There are lots of different kinds of blood in our family. But here in the United States, the word 'Negro' is used to mean anyone who has any Negro blood at all in his veins. In Africa, the word is more pure. It means all Negro, therefore black. I am brown."

Henry Louis Gates Jr. is the scholar who hosts the PBS *African American Lives* and *Faces of America*, in which he uses historical documents and DNA to trace the genealogies of famous African Americans. Gates reveals that "the average African American is 77 percent black and 20 percent white."[2]

What are you?

Research your family history and/or genealogy. Record your findings and share them in a report or oral presentation.

With a Friend

Find an older member of a minority group and interview him or her. It is important to choose an older person who has had many decades of experiences. With your friend, develop a list of questions to ask that will help you decide if your community is less prejudiced of this people group than it was years ago.

What if you don't know anyone of a different ethnic culture or race than yours? Many cities have ethnic groups that your library can help you find. You may also want to check the phone book for local churches whose membership is composed of a race or nationality different from yours. Visit a restaurant with an international flavor—Chinese, Thai, or Indian—and ask a worker to introduce you to someone of that nationality.

After you have done your interview, report your findings to an interested listener. Hopefully, you will have made a new friend of a different culture, too.

I'll Watch the Movie

Pudd'nhead Wilson was made into a movie in 1983. It starred Ken Howard as Pudd'nhead. The scriptwriter moved some plot points around and omitted others. View the movie and note the differences. Determine which you like better—the movie or the book. Decide whether the changes make the story better. Give a movie review in which you reveal the movie's merits and flaws but not the ending!

Or try the 1927, 1929, 1936, or 1951 version of *Show Boat*, all based on Edna Ferber's bestselling book *Show Boat*. The book and the movies address racial prejudice in the 1880s along the Mississippi River. Write a review of any of them or make a video review.

You're the Expert

Research one of the following subjects and write a short report (400-1,000 words) on it:

- Fingerprinting—history, techniques, patterns, uses, etc.
- Twins—ones that have grown up together or have been separated at a young age; include an interview with a twin or a set of twins, if possible
- Conjoined twins—formerly called "Siamese twins"
- Blood—find the differences, if any, between the bloods of different races

Sometimes I Feel like a Motherless Child

Negro spirituals (or just "spirituals") are powerful songs that express deep feelings about life's events and troubles. Research these songs, learn some, and perform them for your class. Or perhaps you would like to write one of your own and perform it for the class. Here are two sites to get you started: http://www.negrospirituals.com and http://thenegrospiritualinc.com.

Double the Trouble

Sam Clemens had an interest in twins and changelings, and it appears in his books. But he isn't the only one interested in switched or dual personalities. The movie *Freaky Friday* is based on the switched personalities of a mother and daughter. Oscar Wilde's *The Importance of Being Earnest* plays with the idea of a man using one persona in the city and one in the country. These are interesting ways to look at what happens when people switch places with each other or create double personalities (as Sam Clemens did when he created the persona of Mark Twain).

Write a short story or play in which twins or other people switch places for a while. What trouble will they encounter? Will they get back to normal?

Unrelated

Sam Clemens' three daughters often asked him to make up stories for them, and he liked to oblige. One way in which he created stories was to look at the items on the mantelpiece and incorporate each piece, from left to right, into the story. His daughters were delighted with this method and would not let him deviate from the order of the items. I wonder how many stories he told using those same five or six items (a vase, a picture frame, a candlestick, etc.).

Your mission is to collect five totally unrelated items and place them in front of you. If it would be more interesting to have someone else gather the items and surprise you, then by all means, ask them to.

The next part of the mission is to write a short story using all of those items. Incorporate them into the story in any way you like and use them in any order.

If you are feeling brave, write the story with your non-dominant hand, just as Mark Twain taught himself to do when he developed arthritis. In other words, if you are right handed, write with your left.

Black Is Beautiful

Investigate famous African Americans or international blacks. Create a list of three African Americans and their accomplishments and report your findings to an interested listener. Or create a list of three blacks from any country and their accomplishments and report your findings to an interested listener.

History Buff

Research the history of blacks in America and create a timeline. These might get you started: the Supreme Court's 1857 Dred Scott decision, the Missouri Compromise, the Thirteenth and Fourteenth Amendments, *Brown v. the Board of Education of Topeka* (1954), and the Voting Rights Act of 1965. The *Brown v. the Board of Education of Topeka* case has particular interest to this year of literature because the Supreme Court's decision in this case was the major factor in the book you will read soon, *Warriors Don't Cry.*

If you do not live in America or would rather research another topic, try racism, famous blacks, the origin of races, the differences in human blood, modern-day slavery, or the link between racism and Planned Parenthood. Below are some resources to start you out:

"The Ascent of Racism" by Paul Humber
http://www.icr.org/article/ascent-racism/

"Where Did the Races Come From?" by John D. Morris
http://www.icr.org/article/1062/

"It's not just Black and White" by Ken Ham, an article about the origin of the races and about multicolored twins
http://www.answersingenesis.org/articles/am/v3/n2/twins-black-and-white

Maafa 21: *Black Genocide in 21st Century America*, a documentary on black genocide and Planned Parenthood
http://maafa21.com/

Modern-day slavery
http://www.infoplease.com/spot/slavery1.html

Teacher, the grading grid for *Pudd'nhead Wilson* is on the next page. The grid is marked for a possible 100 points per book. Please feel free to adjust it to your needs and expectations. You have permission to copy it as many times as needed for your own class, co-op, reading group, book-of-the-month club, or family.

Grading grid for *Pudd'nhead Wilson*

Student Name: _____

Online "Yes, I read it" quiz, graded online. 1-10 points	
Online literary terms quiz, graded online. 1-10 points	
Participation in opinion questions online. 1-10 points	
Quality of participation in discussions. 1-20 points	
Successful completion of lessons and assignments. 1-20 points	
Successful completion of activity. 1-10 points	
Finished reading the book. 1-20 points.	
Total grade for *Pudd'nhead Wilson*	

Writing with Sharon Watson

Chapter 2: *The War of the Worlds*

Dover Publications   ISBN: 0-486-29506-0

Facebook Posts

If your group or co-op meets monthly, you may want to keep in touch with the students and keep them interested in the novels by creating a secret Facebook group for only them and their parents. Below are the questions I've asked my Facebook group. Feel free to devise your own questions or find your own links to interesting material.

- Welcome to *The War of the Worlds* by H. G. Wells! Watch this short video from YouTube to give you an idea of what Wells saw as he planned his Martian invasion. Our guide takes us from the direction of Horsell (pronounced HOR-zl) Common, mentioned in the book. Have fun imagining the Martian landing in this sandpit! http://www.youtube.com/watch?v=mn1WMuPzRUY

- The infamous *War of the Worlds* radio broadcast is over 75 years old. Orson Welles' use of "reality" fiction as Martians landed in Grover's Mills, New Jersey, is examined in depth in this show: http://www.pbs.org/wgbh/americanexperience/films/worlds/. Watch it and tell us something that surprises you about the show or the original radio broadcast.

- H.G. Wells often compares humans to animals in *The War of the Worlds*. The first time he does this is on page 1: To the Martians, we must be like the "transient creatures that swarm and multiply in a drop of water." The next comparison to animals is on page 2: "And we men, the creatures who inhabit this earth, must be to them [the Martians] at least as alien and lowly as are the monkeys and lemurs to us." In other words, his analogy is that men are to Martians as monkeys are to men. What animals does Wells compare us to? Why do you think he constantly uses these similes and metaphors to compare us to animals? In what ways is his analogy correct? In what ways does his analogy not work?

- What would you do if your town or neighborhood was invaded by terrorists, Martians, or zombies?

- In *The War of the Worlds*, the artilleryman says the women of the future should be "able-bodied, clean-minded women we want also--mothers and teachers. No lackadaisical ladies--no blasted rolling eyes. We can't have any weak or silly. . . . the useless and cumbersome and mischievous have to die. They ought to die. They ought to be willing to die. It's a sort of disloyalty, after all, to live and taint the race." He believes, as did H. G. Wells, that to have a rightful place in society, women should be useful: solid-thinking mothers and teachers. They have to do something for society, something society values, not just be "cumbersome and mischievous." This is the philosophy of utilitarianism where people believe you must be useful or you have no place in the culture. While this seems wonderful, it discounts all the sick folks and others who are deemed to be "not contributing to society." Where does our culture exhibit this idea of utilitarianism today? Give examples of "You must be useful or you are nothing or worthless or don't deserve to live."

- What question would you like to ask H. G. Wells?

Before You Read the Book

Students who complete reading *The War of the Worlds* will appreciate a small reward. Let the reward refer to something in the book and let students guess what it refers to. Ideas for small reward:

- lollipops (referring to the Lick Observatory mentioned on page 3 of *The War of the Worlds*)
- Mars chocolate bars or Milky Way bars

Lesson 1

Your World—Smashed

Teacher, students are responding to a scenario in which people come into their homes and take over their families.

Write down three words to describe how you might feel or what you would do if this happened to you. Use the space below. *Answers will vary.*

Think of a time in your city, region, or country when people might have felt this way. Think of a time when you experienced a war, natural disaster, or other kind of upheaval that had you wondering what would happen next. How did you feel at the time? Who in the world might be feeling this way now? Write your answers in the space below: *Answers will vary. Victims of ISIS or other militant Muslim groups, victims of regime changes, survivors of natural disasters or wars, and so forth.*

Suggested Reading and Homework Plan: Preview

Teacher, below is the schedule your students are following. Please let them know if you expect them to use another schedule and tell them when the activity is due.

Week 1:
  ❑ Complete lessons 1-3.
Week 2:
  ❑ Read Book I (chapters I – XVII) of *The War of the Worlds*.

Week 3:
  ❑ Read Book II (chapters I – X) of *The War of the Worlds*.

Week 4:

- ❑ Decide on one activity and begin work on it. You'll find the list of activities at the end of this chapter. **Your teacher will tell you when this is due.**
- ❑ Complete lessons 4-7.
- ❑ Hand in your activity and go to your happy place.

Imitate!

Objectives:
- To learn the term *assonance* and identify it in a paragraph.
- To imitate good writing by using one paragraph from *The War of the Worlds* as the template (vivid verbs and assonance).

Turn to page 78 in *The War of the Worlds* ("The Exodus from London") and study the paragraph that begins "There were sad, haggard women tramping by . . . ."

Wells keeps this paragraph from being a boring list of refugees by using **vivid verbs**. These folks are tramping, stumbling, smothered, and smeared. They are thrusting and struggling, not merely walking. This is effective writing because it paints such a graphic word picture for readers and brings the scene alive with movement.

In addition, he uses the *sounds* of the words to create a picture for us. When he writes that "their weary faces [were] smeared with tears," he is using **assonance**, the repetition of internal vowels—in this case, the "ear" sound. He uses three different assonance patterns in that sentence. What are they and what effect does the use of assonance have on the meaning of the sentence? *"Sad, haggard women tramping" and "smothered in dust." By its lyricism, it elevates those sufferers from mere dirty refugees to human beings who find themselves in unaccustomed cataclysmic events.*

Copy out that paragraph and then rewrite it by using its structure. Remove all the adjectives, nouns, and verbs and add your own. Instead of folks escaping from London, how about shoppers rushing a store early Friday morning after Thanksgiving or travelers fleeing a train accident?

Your "skeleton" will look something like the sentence below, with all the adjectives, nouns, and verbs take out. Now you're ready to create your own scene. Here's the first sentence. Adapt it to your description:

There were _____, _____ _____
_____ by, _____ _____, with
_____ that _____ and _____,
their _____ _____ _____ in _____,
their _____ _____ _____ with
_____.

Teacher: If you have time in class, you may want to use this as an in-class writing opportunity so students can learn by what their peers have written. If you are teaching a co-op, the paragraph can be due in a week or emailed to you.

Lesson 2

Meet Mr. Wells

Objective: To discover how much of H. G. Wells' life experiences and beliefs influence *The War of the Worlds*.

Write two things about his life that you find interesting: *Answers will vary.*

Fun Fact

Students may want to go to https://www.youtube.com/watch?v=Xs0K4ApWl4g so they can watch (listen to) Orson Welles' famous radio version of *The War of the Worlds* broadcast in 1938.

Genre and Setting

The genre for this novel is science-fiction (sci-fi or SF).

In the space below, write the names of other science-fiction books you've read or authors you've enjoyed: *Answers will vary.*

A book's setting consists of the time and the place of the story. On page three of *The War of the Worlds*, the protagonist tells the reader how many years ago all this happened. How many years ago was it? Fill in the blank: *6 years*. In what year was this story first published? Fill in the blank: *1898*

Point of View

The War of the Worlds is told in **first-person point of view** (POV). The main character is never named, but we know he's a married male. The chapters "In London," "The Exodus from London," and "The 'Thunder Child'" are told in **first-person peripheral POV** because the narrator is not the main character in those chapters. Our normal protagonist tells us about the experiences of his brother George in London; he stands on the periphery and tells the story from there.

Too Good to Forget

Mark any passages you especially liked or didn't like, that you found interesting or well written. Or enter them in your Novel Notebook for future reference. If you want to remember a long passage, you may want to type it into a special file on your computer instead of using your Novel Notebook.

To download a FREE Novel Notebook with the questions already in it, go to http://writingwithsharonwatson.com/illuminating-literature-when-worlds-collide-gateway/ .

Lesson 3

Writers' Device: Reaction

Objectives:
- To understand how a character's reaction can color the way a reader views the event or another character.
- To understand that the author is "that man behind the curtain," pulling the strings of the story and manipulating characters and events.

Students are learning the importance of a reaction after a story event. It shapes how the author wants the reader to view the event.

Here's an example of Wells trying to head off an "Eewww!" reaction from readers. Turn to page 100 ("What We Saw from the Ruined House") and read his description of the gory eating habits of the Martians. Then read the short paragraph just after that. Wells tries to desensitize the reader to the repulsiveness of the Martians by using the lead's reactions. How does Wells do it? Write your answer below. *He appeals to our sense of fairness and logic by comparing the reader's reaction to the goriness of the Martians' eating habits to how a rabbit might be repulsed by our eating meat. In other words, the main character reasoned that if we do it and it seems okay, we ought to cut the Martians a little slack; maybe they're not so bad after all but only following their natural evolutionary bent, just as we are. Wells tamps down any gross reactions by becoming cerebral and logical and by suggesting, "Hey, if we do it, it must be okay for the Martians to do it."*

Literary Terms: Alliteration and Allusion

Objective: To learn and identify the literary terms *alliteration* and *allusion*.

Alliteration When two or more words in close proximity begin with the same consonant sound. <u>F</u>ierce <u>f</u>ight, <u>d</u>evastatingly <u>d</u>ivine <u>d</u>essert, <u>p</u>ink <u>p</u>arasol—all of these are alliterations.

Allusion When an author refers to something without giving an explanation. The "something" an author refers to is often from Shakespeare, Greek or Roman mythology, a historical reference, or the Bible. For instance, if one character is so endangered that he says he's under the sword of Damocles, he is referring to the sword from Greek mythology placed point down and hung by a hair directly over someone's head. The tension is so strong because the hair could break at any moment.

Your Novel Notebook

Objectives:
- To train students to be active readers.
- To list references to evolution to discover how evolutionary thinking affects what the protagonist does and feels.
- To list the protagonist's reactions to and descriptions of the curate as a means to seeing the author's negative opinion of God and Christianity and how these negative reactions can color our perception of Christianity as well.

Teacher, below is the list of items your students will be compiling in their Novel Notebooks. You may want to discuss or review these with your students or simply ask to see their notebooks to make sure they compiled the lists. Adjust this list to your needs. *Answers are located in the Questions for Discussion section.*

- List 1: Three passages that show evolutionary thinking
- List 2: The main character's reactions to and descriptions of the curate (a clergyman)
- List 3: The dangers or troubles the main character encounters
- One example of alliteration
- One allusion

To download a FREE Novel Notebook with the questions already in it, go to http://writingwithsharonwatson.com/illuminating-literature-when-worlds-collide-gateway/ .

This is the end of lesson 3. Now on to *The War of the Worlds* . . .

Suggested Reading and Homework Plan

Week 1:
- ❑ Complete lessons 1-3. Complete any unfinished Week 1 tasks now.

Week 2:
- ❑ Read Book I (chapters I – XVII) of *The War of the Worlds*.

Week 3:
- ❑ Read Book II (chapters I – X) of *The War of the Worlds*.

Week 4:
- ❑ Decide on one activity and begin work on it. You'll find the list of activities at the end of this chapter. **Your teacher will tell you when this is due.**
- ❑ Complete lessons 4-7.
- ❑ Hand in your activity and go to your happy place.

Stuff You Might Want to Know: Chapter by Chapter

Teacher, this subheading contains definitions and facts to clarify some of the events that occur in *The War of the Worlds,* things to make the novel easier to understand.

After You've Read the Book

Lesson 4

Reward: Lollipops (the Lick Observatory mentioned on page 3 of *The War of the Worlds*), Mars chocolate bars, or the fun-size Milky Way candy bars.

Five-Star Report

Students are filling out a graphic, giving *The War of the Worlds* a rating (1 = Couldn't stand it; 5 = Loved it!) based on how they feel about it. If students have a strong reaction to the book, you may want to ask why. *Answers will vary.*

Why do you think *The War of the Worlds* is considered a classic? List two reasons here: *Answers will vary.*

Complete the Online Quizzes and Opinion Survey

Objectives:
- To complete a short fact quiz online for a grade to prove students read the book.
- To reinforce the terms they've learned so far in this text: allusion, alliteration, assonance, genre, reaction, conflict, protagonist, antagonist, and *nom de plume* (pseudonym).
- To complete questions online to express opinions, interpret events in *The War of the Worlds*, and ponder what they would do in similar circumstances.

The password to the quizzes and survey is WELLS.

Teacher, students are instructed to go to this address to get links to take the quizzes: http://WritingWithSharonWatson.com/illuminating-literature-when-worlds-collide-gateway/ .
- "Yes, I read it" quiz—graded online for you
- Literary Terms Quiz (allusion, alliteration, assonance, genre, reaction, conflict, protagonist, antagonist, and *nom de plume* [pseudonym])—graded online for you
- Opinion Survey—no grade, but answers to the opinion questions may help you develop a strategy for your discussion time.

THESE QUIZZES ARE FREE. Students are allowed two attempts for the quizzes and one for the opinion survey. Also, the quiz site will email a full report of the quiz (questions, your student's answers, the correct answers, and your student's grade) to the email address your student signed in with.

Teacher, if you prefer printed quizzes, you'll find them in *Illuminating Literature: When Worlds Collide, Quiz and Answer Manual*, available for sale at http://writingwithsharonwatson.com/illuminating-literature-when-worlds-collide.

Even if the quiz site gives a grade for this opinion survey, it is not graded. The only grade students receive for this survey is one for participation. The answers your students give to these questions may help you formulate what you would like to discuss in class with them.

Vocabulary Quizzola for *The War of the Worlds*

Objectives:
- To reinforce good vocabulary habits and awareness.
- To gain a grade separate from the Grading Grid.

Directions: Match the definition on the right to the correct word on the left. Write the letter in the blank next to the word. Page numbers in parentheses are from the Dover Thrift Edition. **Ask your teacher if this is an open-book quiz.** Each correct answer is worth 5 points.

L__1. Sham (104)	A. howling
G__2. Attenuated (2)	B. upcoming, just about to happen
C__3. Putrescent (134)	C. rotting
K__4. Gloaming (19)	D. unenergetic, lacking energy
Q__5. Conflagration (37)	E. corrupted, made impure
J__6. Colossus (48)	F. false rumor, crazy bit of news
S__7. Gesticulating (107)	G. thin and/or drawn out
A__8. Ululation (65)	H. of Earth
N__9. Din (81)	I. the skin or a covering
D__10. Lethargic (92)	J. giant
P__11. Fortnight (94)	K. a glow after sunset
I__12. Integument (99)	L. fake, pretend
T__13. Carmine (103)	M. of the night
H__14. Terrestrial (1)	N. lots of noise
M__15. Nocturnal (56)	O. the highest point
O__16. Zenith (6)	P. two weeks (14 days)
F__17. Canard (24)	Q. a large fire
B__18. Imminent (55)	R. center of a fortification
E__19. Vitiated (105)	S. wildly gesturing
R__20. Redoubt (136)	T. red

Total number correct: _____
Vertical word encoded in correct answers: *SANDPIT*

Lesson 5

Colliding Worlds

Objective:
- To list the worlds that collide in *The War of the Worlds*.
- To draw conclusions about the collisions.

So, what worlds are colliding with each other? What worlds are at war? What people, philosophies, or cultures were in conflict with each other? Think in terms of actual physical conflict or conflicts of philosophy and worldview. Fill in the list below. The first one is done for you.

1. The Martians collide with the Earthlings.
2. *Evolution collides with Creation.*
3. *Religion (in the character of the curate) collides with science, logic, saneness, and reason (in the character of the protagonist).*
4. *Morality collides with expediency.*
5. *Self-preservation collides with compassion (in the character of the protagonist's brother George).*
6. *Students will think of other collisions.*

Teacher, students are now drawing conclusions based on their lists. They are using these two questions:

What negative things happen when these worlds collide? Write your answer: *mayhem, disruption of society, murder, disruption of families, cessation of industry and livelihoods, self-preservation is utmost in some people's minds, Christianity is shown for the weak religion it is (in the author's mind), people feel demoralized, and so forth.*

What positive things happen when these worlds collide? Write your answer: *People come together to help each other, determination to beat the foe, heroic deeds, and so on.*

Conflicts

Objective: To list the lead's conflicts in *The War of the Worlds*.

Fill in the spaces below with the specific conflicts the protagonist faces in *The War of the Worlds*. If you have already done this in your Novel Notebook, rejoice! There is no need to do it again here

Teacher: Some of these conflicts can go into more than one category. For instance, the Heat-Ray can represent another character, as it is used by the Martians, or it can be categorized as technology. The important thing here is to see the variety of antagonistic forces aligned against the narrator.

1. The lead against himself. (The numbers indicate the page number in the Dover Thrift Edition of *The War of the Worlds*.)
Fear, 18
Anxious for his wife, 91
Fierce with fear, 111
Loneliness, 133

Lonely and sad at losing his wife, 139
Terror, a horror of his own temerity, 135
For three days, he suffered a reaction to trauma: "I drifted—a demented man," which,
you will note, is acceptable behavior for him but not for the curate, 138-9

2. The lead against another character.
The Martian Heat-Ray almost gets him, 17
The Heat-Ray reaches his chimney and house, 29
Tries to get rid of the curate but can't, 93
Trapped in a house with the curate (with whom his is "incompatible"), 95 and 105
The curate (eats too much, talks too loudly, acts stupidly), Book the Second, Chapters 3-4
Strikes the curate with the blunt end of a meat chopper, 111
One Martian comes looking for him, 111-113

3. The lead against society.
The Martians in their tripod machines, striding en masse *across the country 33-4*
The Martians' strategy, 83
The Martians set up a headquarters outside the house, 95
The Martians are going to set up human farms to feed themselves, "The man on Putney
*   Hill"*

4. The lead against nature.
Thunderstorm and hail, 33
The boiling water in the river, 50
Intense weariness and fever, 52
The Black Smoke, 68
Near starvation, 105
Starving, dehydrated, 113-4

5. The lead against God/the gods/fate. (*This is more subtle; he does not raise his fist at*
God outright.)
His elaborate justifications in whacking the curate with the meat chopper, 106, 110-1,
119; his negative reactions against everything the curate says and does is symbolic of his
fight against God, Christianity, and religion.

6. The lead against technology/biotechnology
Heat-Ray
Black Smoke
The mining efforts of the Martians when the lead and the curate are stuck in the
abandoned house
The lead's conversation with "the man on Putney Hill" as they discuss eugenics, only
allowing the "fit" to live and reproduce. Although the lead does not feel a conflict here,
he does encounter the heading of "biotechnology."

44

Lesson 6

Writers' Device: Empathetic Character

Objectives:
- To learn how authors create empathetic characters so that even questionable actions appear necessary and advantageous.
- To learn to look for this device so students can be more discerning readers.

When the protagonist uses the dull edge of the meat chopper to whack the pesky, losing-his-mind curate on the neck, readers may believe the action is justified because, after all, readers are naturally on the side of the protagonist. We want him to be safe. We feel he was justified; he had to do it, unsuspecting readers might feel. What are the passages that lead us to this conclusion?

First, the lead tells us this: "It is disagreeable for me to recall and write these things." Because he is the protagonist and is troubled, we have empathy toward him and applaud his honesty. This is the "I have agonized over this decision" ploy.

Second, he tells us that the curate is now insane; the author makes the curate a bumbling and dangerous fool. Remember that it is the author who is hiding behind the scenes, pulling the characters' strings. Things are not just happening; the writer is the puppeteer. Wells creates the curate as being on the edge of reason so it will be inevitable that the lead has to silence him.

Third, after whacking the curate, the narrator himself is in mortal danger from the Martians. Putting the lead in jeopardy is an effective method for creating empathy for him. Instantly, he is justified in his action, and the reader is on his side when the lead becomes the victim, fighting for his life.

*Fourth, he explains to the reader that he was driven toward it step by step, a "creature of a sequence of accidents leading inevitably to that." This is the "I am all out of options" strategy. Additionally, authors consciously **narrow down the options** the protagonist has at the crucial time.*

Locate one passage in which the narrator paints the curate as stupid, weak or bumbling. In the space below, write out the author's description of the curate or his actions. This description becomes one justification for readers having no empathy for that character. *Students may use excerpts from chapters "How I Fell in with the Curate," "Under Foot," "What We Saw from the Ruined House," "The Days of Imprisonment," and "The Death of the Curate" in which the curate is painted as a blathering, whimpering, going-insane, dangerous man.* How did *you* feel about the curate? *Answers will vary.*

To put this into perspective, let's play What If. What if the curate had really been a lovely woman? Do you think the lead would have been so quick to dispense with her to save his own hide? What if the other character had been a little kid or a dog or his wife or his life-long friend?

When viewed in this light, we can see that the narrator let his negative reactions to the curate color his actions.

Remember: Things do not just happen in stories. There's always a man (or woman) behind that curtain, pulling the levers and making things occur.

Lesson 7

Questions for Discussion

Objectives:
- To discuss important topics touched on in *The War of the Worlds*: eugenics, negative view of Christianity, reaction to invasion.
- To learn to look at these topics through the lens of the Bible.

Teacher: There is no way you can discuss all these questions in class! Choose any of the questions or topics below that apply to your needs, your class time, and your students.

Teacher, ask students these questions to get the discussion going:

1. What questions do you have about *The War of the Worlds*?
2. What aspects of this book appealed to you?
3. What is your impression of this book?

These preliminary questions will help to clear up any misunderstandings or miscomprehensions from the stories, and they'll get students talking during the discussion session. Students can answer other students' questions, too. This pre-discussion time may also serve to answer some of the questions printed below or can be a springboard to any of the aspects of the book you want to focus on.

Teacher, these questions are for discussion or for writing assignments. Feel free to choose the ones you feel will be most helpful to your teens. In addition, after reading the responses your teens entered in *The War of the Worlds* Opinion Survey, you might want to adjust your discussion time according to what you find there.

Follow-up for the Novel Notebook lists:
1. Three passages that show evolutionary thinking. *Some references to evolution in the Dover Thrift Edition: Mars older than Earth (1), one is vain to believe life exists only on Earth (2), "inferior races" (3), "organic evolution" (5), need for sleep shows inferiority because Earthlings have not evolved (101), and sexual*

adaptations (101), natural selection (102), Earthlings are behind Martians on the evolutionary scale (103-4), "sense of dethronement" at being merely an animal (116), natural selection and adaptations (117), he feels like "an inferior animal" (120), humans are powerless to change (124), survival of the fittest (127), "prehuman ancestors" and "natural selection" (136), "petty surface of our minute sphere" (144).

2. What are the main character's reactions to/descriptions of the curate? How do they color your view of the curate and his actions? *He has a weak face, a retreating chin to indicate weakness, and blankly staring eyes. He looks vacant, has a thin white hand and a complaining tone. The protagonist can only stare at him when the curate asks rhetorical questions (53). He speaks like one demented, repeats himself, quotes Scripture with flaming eyes (54). The protagonist says the curate is on "the very edge of his reason" and commands him to "Be a man!" while the protagonist speaks matter-of-factly (54). He contrasts his own logical anxieties for his wife with the curate's unreasonably selfish despair (91). When the lead wants to escape, the curate is "lethargic, unreasonable" (92). The unmanly curate whimpers to himself and crawls after the protagonist (96-7). He has a "stupid rigidity of mind," talks in "endless muttering monologue," and eats more than the protagonist thinks he should (105). They fight and bicker, threaten each other and come to blows (106). The curate is "incapable of discussion," has no "reason or forethought," has "sunk to the level of an animal," and "would...fail me" (108). "He was beyond reason," gluttonous, and "a man insane" (110). Many of the descriptions of the curate are in glaring and direct contrast to the protagonist's own actions and thoughts, which is an effective writer's device. When the protagonist becomes angry or anxious, it seems logical, as when he describes himself as "a demented man" (139). When the curate becomes anxious, it seems overblown and selfish. These reactions and descriptions may persuade readers to agree with the protagonist when he says he had to whack the curate, that he was justified in shutting him up. They may also persuade readers to believe that men of the cloth (churchmen) or Christians are hypocritical or, at the least, are of no help in times of crisis, which mirrors Well's belief that God is "an ever absent help in times of trouble."[3]***Most likely, these reactions and descriptions accumulate to put the curate, and thus Christianity, in a negative light in the eyes of the student.***

3. The dangers or troubles the main character encounters. *See Conflicts under After You've Read the Book section of this chapter's answer key. Students may have answered this already in their Novel Notebooks as well.*

4. One alliteration *"frantic, fantastic" (22), "monstrous beings of metal moving" (35), "whirling white" (49), "sudden, dreadful, and destructive . . . that destroyed" (51), "tripod towers" (137).*

5. One allusion **Teacher, you may want to discuss how the allusions affect the meaning of the part of the story where they are found. Examples follow:** *Gorgon (14) alludes to mythological female monsters who had snakes in their hair or snakes for hair—very creepy! "Fishers of men" (28) alludes to Jesus' remark to new disciples in Matthew 4:19. Titan (40, 86, 117) refers to*

early gods of Greek mythology, some of which were Gaea (Earth), Uranus (Sky), Oceanus (bodies of water), and connotes something large or powerful. Pillars of fire and "bloodshot smoke" (41) refers to the biblical pillars of fire and smoke that accompanied the Hebrew slaves as they fled from Egypt. "The smoke of her burning" (54) refers to Revelation 18:9 and the destruction of Babylon. The "great and terrible day of the Lord" (54) and the falling mountains and rocks (54) allude to Joel 2:31 and Revelation 6:16, respectively; the curate knew the end-time verses of destruction but didn't know how to apply them or how to react in a godly manner. The "destruction of Pompeii" (92) alludes to the Roman town in what is now Italy that was buried in volcanic eruptions and ash in AD 79. "Lilienthal soaring machines" (103) alludes to Otto Lilienthal, an early aviation pioneer who had success with gliders. Its "Briareus of a handling-machine" (112) alludes to some important anatomical features of this Greek god who had one hundred hands and fifty heads; sounds pretty handy—and frightening to onlookers! The "mechanical Samson" (134) alludes to the strongman Samson of the Bible. The "destruction of Sennacherib" (136-7) alludes to the historical account recorded in 2 Kings 18-19 in which God rescues Jerusalem under Hezekiah's reign by sending an angel to kill Sennacherib's army by stealth of night.

These questions might help clear things up a bit as well:

1. What is the main character's name? *The main character (protagonist) has no name. Wells wants him to represent reason, logic, and forward-thinking scientific men who want to create a new society based on reason and science, not religion. It also gives the character an "everyman" feel.*

2. How does the reader know what goes on in London while the narrator is somewhere else? *He gets his information later from his brother George, who was a medical student in London, and from newspapers. Students may remember that our author's middle name is George and that he had been a medical student in London.*

3. How do the Martians die? *By earthly bacteria.*

Questions on the topic of eugenics. Here is a scary article on eugenics and related topics: http://www.chesterton.org/lecture-36/

1. Eugenics is, basically, allowing reproduction among only those humans who are deemed fit or are viewed as contributing members of society, in an effort to improve a certain human population by use of "good genes." Often the flip side of the coin is that those deemed unfit are not allowed to reproduce or are destroyed so they cannot reproduce. As the artilleryman declares, "They ought to die." Find the reference to eugenics and write down the page number. *Page 127.* Taking into consideration the artilleryman's criteria,

would you be one of those people he would allow to reproduce? Why or why not? *Answers will vary.*

2. Compare and contrast the artilleryman's plan to allow only "able-bodied, clean-minded" men and women a chance to survive versus God's mandate to "administer true justice; show mercy and compassion to one another. Do not oppress the widow or the fatherless, the alien or the poor. In your heart, do not think evil of each other" (Zechariah 7: 9-10). *Answers will vary.*

3. Do you agree with the artilleryman that "weak or silly" people have no right to live? Do you agree with his assessment that they are disloyal to humanity if they reproduce and "taint the race"? Is it true that "weak or silly" people "can't be happy" (127)? *Answers will vary.*

4. In what ways would the soul of a nation be affected if it killed members of its society deemed misfits or non-contributing members of society? Give one example from history. *Answers will vary.*

Questions on the topic of Wells' negative view of religion and Christianity:

1. What steps does Wells take to present the curate in a negative light? *He gives him a weak face, receding chin, whiny voice, makes him complaining, can't deal with reality, spouts Scripture with seemingly no sense of what it means or that it can mean anything, makes him like a leech to the lead, gives him so sense of self-preservation or sense of protecting others when both men are in the house next to the Martians, the curate gets the lead into life-threatening trouble due to his inability to cope with the invasion.*

2. What do you think the lead would have done if the other character in the abandoned house had been a beautiful woman, a kid, dog, or his wife? *Answers will vary; most likely, he would have leaned toward mercy or toward finding another solution to his problem other than whacking.*

3. Wells sets the curate up as being a sham of a Christian. How does the curate not represent true Christians and Christianity? Create a Christian character who really does represent Christianity. *Answers will vary.*

4. While Wells presents evolution in a positive light, he is negative about some human biological functions. What three things about humans does he put in a negative light, physical things to which the Martians are superior? *Digestion, sleeping patterns, reproductive methods*

Questions on the topic of reacting to an invasion:

1. What is the inherent meaning in the Martians' landing in a common? *Wells may be saying that an invasion (any attack of any sort) belongs to all of us; it is a problem belonging to all of us and we must all work together to solve it.*

2. "He was a lucky man to have friends" (79). This is said of a bleeding man being helped by two friends by the side of the road. In what ways have you helped a friend in a calamity? In what ways have others helped you? In what ways do you think you might be useful to others in a time of trouble? *Answers will vary.*

3. Describe a catastrophe you have experienced. What helped you get through it? *Answers will vary.*

Teacher, here are some extra questions you may want to consider:

1. Why do you think the protagonist often compares humans to animals, as when folks in the river scramble out "like little frogs hurrying through the grass from the advance of a man" (50)? How is this related to Kepler's quotation at the beginning of the book? Why does Wells continually make the Martians' attack analogous to our treatment of animals? *It shows that Wells believed we are all animals, doing what we are predisposed to do by nature. A partial list of the different animals to which the author compares humans: bacteria and other denizens of a drop of water (1), men are to Martians as monkeys and lemurs are to men (2), extinct dodo bird (24), little frogs (50), a disturbed hive of bees (67), wasps (70), ants (48, 123, 139), rabbits (116), a rat (120).* **Teacher,** *check out Kepler's quotation before* The War of the Worlds *table of contents.*

2. *Answers will vary.*

3. What is your reaction to the following passage spoken by the lead? "What good is religion if it collapses under calamity? Think of what earthquakes and floods, wars and volcanoes, have done before to men! [God] is not an insurance agent" (54). Do you agree or disagree with the lead? *Answers will vary.*

4. How true to the facts is Wells' presentation of evolution throughout the story? *Answers will vary.*

5. "It ain't no murder killing beasts like that" (28). What constitutes murder?

6. The lead smacks the curate across the neck with the butt of a meat chopper. The curate falls and, according to the lead, "lay still." After the lead runs to the coal cellar, he hears a "heavy body" being dragged across the floor. He peeks through the door to see a Martian "scrutinizing the curate's head." In your opinion, who killed the curate: the lead or the Martian? How important is self-preservation? *Answers will vary.*

7. In your opinion and based on what you know of the characters, if the Martians had lived longer and had set up their human farms, which of the characters would have complied with the plan? *Answers will vary.*

8. If you could create a new character to respond to some of the events in the story, who would it be and how would he/she be different from ones in the story? *Answers will vary.*

9. Is the lead morally responsible for the curate's death? Why or why not? *Answers will vary; one hopes students will choose "yes."*

10. What are the main character's beliefs about a God? Are his actions consistent with his beliefs? *Most of these beliefs are shown in the way the main character treats, views, and writes about the curate—in other words, God and religion are not capable of dealing with the hard realities of life and will not be there in your time of need. His actions are not consistent with his beliefs. On page 112 he "prays copiously," and on page 138 he raises his hands and "began thanking God." The main character is, by literal definition, a hypocrite.*

11. The man on Putney Hill (the artilleryman) has some ideas of how to begin civilization over again. What are they? How would you begin civilization over again? *He espouses eugenics: "Able-bodied, clean-minded" women will mother the new race. All other women move over and die because they are of no use in the new society. "Weaklings" and "rubbish" will not be allowed to live long enough to father the new race. Basically, it's survival of the fittest. They'll live underground, coming out only when the Martians aren't around. Someone will capture a few Martians and learn to use the Heat-Ray. They will gather books—useful science books, not fiction—to learn and to keep science alive (126-7).*

If You Liked This Book . . .

Students are viewing a list of books similar to *The War of the Worlds* in genre.

What other books or short stories would you add to this list? Write them below: *Answers will vary.*

This is the end of lesson 7.

Your Choice of Activities

Objectives:
- To choose and complete one activity and share the results with the class, group, or interested party.
- To actively participate in the topics, themes, and issues of *The War of the Worlds*.

Note: Choose only one of the following activities. Read all of them carefully before you make your decision. **Check with your teacher to see when this is due.**

> Mars—facts on the planet
> With a Friend—your own blueprint for rebuilding civilization after a cataclysmic event
> Choose Your Invader—different types of writing to chronicle your own invasion
> I'll Watch the Movie—viewing movie versions or listening to recorded versions of *The War of the Worlds*
> Write what You Know—using what you already know to write a short story

Reaction Is Powerful—writing an essay on a reaction in *The War of the Worlds* or
    writing a fictional scene with a reaction
Dear Mrs. Wells—a letter of consolation to young Bertie's mother
Dear Bertie—a letter to young Wells

Below are descriptions of the activities. Your teacher will tell you when this assignment is due. Dig in.

Mars

One pages 1, 2, and 23 of *The War of the Worlds*, you will find the scientific facts of the day concerning Mars. Your job is to find out just how correct those facts are and to find new ones. In an essay or list, tell about those facts. For instance, did Mars ever have oceans? Does it have an atmosphere? If so, of what is it composed? Is Wells' statement about gravity correct? Include three facts that scientists know today due to new technology and the Mars rovers Spirit and Opportunity.

Mars is occasionally visible in the night sky. Find out when and where, and view it, if possible.

With a Friend

In the chapter titled "The Man on Putney Hill," Wells has the artilleryman give his ideas on how to rebuild civilization after the Martians have destroyed it. His ideas include eugenics, euthanasia, going off the grid, stockpiling, and a whole host of other methods that he hopes will build a better tomorrow.

So, what's your idea? How would you go about rebuilding civilization after a catastrophe?

Find a friend and come up with a blueprint for rebuilding civilization after some sort of cataclysmic event (comet, disease, earthquake, an EMP attack, enemy army) has wiped out our world as we know it. What will be the rules, and who will make them? What kind of government will you have? How will people communicate with each other? How will they get education? Housing? Food? What will your new society look like?

Choose Your Invader

Teacher, this one is a lot of fun if you divide your class into teams, assign them a method, and have them present the results after 30 minutes.

What would it be like if your town were invaded by something that was bent on conquering the area? In this exercise, you will choose who or what your invader will be—people, countries, animals, strange monsters, diseases—and a method to chronicle the event.

Read the options below and choose one. Then decide if you want to do this alone or write with a friend or a couple of friends. Your project can be anywhere from silly to serious.

1. Choose your invader. Your town and the surrounding areas are being invaded. Write about the invasion as a newspaper or online news site would report it. Do a few daily installments to show the progress of the invasion and its effect on the citizens. Read the articles to an interested listener or publish them for your class or group.

2. Choose your invader. Write about the attack as it might appear in a history book or on the Internet in 10-20 years' time. Read your entry to an interested listener or publish it for your class or group.

3. Choose your invader. Write "breaking news" segments to give people up-to-the-minute accounts of what is happening. Be a TV or radio reporter—you choose. Read these to an interested listener or publish them for your class or group.

4. Choose your invader. You are a personal chronicler, just as the main character in *The War of the Worlds* is and just as Jeremiah the prophet is when he writes his personal account of how Jerusalem fell to the vicious Babylonian army. Will you use journal entries? Letters to someone? Blog posts? Some other way of saving this important information? Write your chronicles of the attacks and what you and others did, and read them to an interested listener or publish them for your class or group.

5. Choose your invader. Just as the biblical prophet Jeremiah is overcome with grief at the fall of Jerusalem and pens Lamentations in response, write a lamentation of your own concerning the attack on your town and the surrounding areas. This is more than a poem; it is a song, a dirge. Write words and music, and sing it to an interested listener or to your class or group.

6. Choose your invader. There are no electronic devices left that work—no videos, cameras, cell phones, radios, tablets, YouTube, Internet, or TVs. Record for posterity what these invaders look like, what the area looks like after the attacks, or actual drawings of the attacks. Be the world's eyes! Present your results to your class or group.

I'll Watch the Movie

The War of the Worlds has been made into a live-radio broadcast and a few movies. Check your local library for the radio or movie versions (the 1953 version is notable). Or for the radio version directed and narrated by Orson Welles and hailed by some as "the most famous broadcast of all time," contact Radio Spirits at http://www.radiospirits.com. Cracker Barrel restaurant occasionally carries the radio version in September and October, just in time for Halloween. And, of course, there's always YouTube: https://www.youtube.com/watch?v=Xs0K4APWl4g.

Secure a copy of either and compare it with the book. What are the differences in the settings? The characters? The philosophies? Which do you like better—the book, the radio version, or the movie?

Write What You Know

If you get very far in writing, you will hear this advice: "Write what you know." H. G. Wells does this quite naturally with his scientific knowledge of biology and zoology and with his interest in futuristic technology. Take a look at the titles of some of his early short stories (the year of publication is in parentheses):

"The Stolen Bacillus" (1894)
"The Flowering of a Strange Orchid" (1894)
"The Triumphs of a Taxidermist" (1894)
"The Moth" (1895)
"The Argonauts of the Air" (1895)
"The Flying Man" (1895)

Another example of the write-what-you-know advice occurs concerning the setting of *The War of the Worlds*. This interesting glimpse into the writer's life is from H. G. Wells' autobiography as he and his wife move into Woking:

> Our withdrawal to Woking was a fairly cheerful adventure. Woking was the site of the first crematorium but few of our friends made more than five or six jokes about that. We . . . furnished a small resolute semi-detached villa with a minute greenhouse in the Maybury Road facing the railway line . . . . Close at hand in those days was a pretty and rarely used canal amidst pine woods, a weedy canal . . . . There I planned and wrote [*The*] *War of the Worlds*, [*The*] *Wheels of Chance* and [*The*] *Invisible Man* . . . . Later on I wheeled about the district marking down suitable places and people for destruction by my Martians.[4]

As you can see, Mr. Wells was very familiar with the setting of his book. He lived in the area and roamed it frequently, often on his bicycle, which was a recent invention. He could have made up the setting entirely in his head, but he decided it would feel more authentic if he used something with which he was familiar. He wrote what he knew about.

Choose a place with which you are very familiar—your neighborhood, a park, the mall, your church, and so forth—and write a short story using that place as your setting. Make something happen there that has never happened there before!

Reaction Is Powerful

The reaction is a powerful tool and can be a negative or positive influence on the reader. For example, it is the Israelite army's reaction—forty days of avoidance and fear—that tells us how formidable an enemy Goliath really is.

Choose a scene in *The War of the Worlds* where a new character is introduced. In a 250-word essay, discuss the reactions of the other characters, what it tells you about the characters, and how a reader might respond to those reactions.

OR

Write a 250-word scene in which a character enters a room. How will the other characters react to him or her? What will this tell the reader about the original characters? About the new character?

Dear Mrs. Wells

Before Bertie was born, his mother lost her only daughter to appendicitis. This was a terrible blow to her, as it would be to any mother. Below is Wells' account of a portion of his mother's life. She was hard working and very poor. When he writes "Our Father" and "Our Saviour," he is being sarcastic. Does he sound angry to you?

> Every night and morning and sometimes during the day she prayed to Our Father and Our Saviour for a little money, for a little leisure, for a little kindness, to make Joe [her husband] better and less negligent—for now he was getting very neglectful of her. It was like writing to an absconding debtor for all the answer she got.
>
> Unless taking away her darling, her wonder, her one sweet and tractable child, her Fanny, her little "Possy," without pity or warning was an answer. A lesson. Fanny was well and happy and then she was flushed and contorted with agony and then in three days she was dead. My mother had to talk to her diary about it. Little boys do not like lamenting mothers; Joe was apt to say, "There, there, Sadie," and go off to his cricket; except for Our Lord and Saviour, whose dumbness, I am afraid, wore the make-believe very thin at times, my mother had to do her weeping alone.[5]

Wells seems to be saying that because of his mother's heartfelt prayers for a little money, leisure, and kindness, God answered meanly by killing off her only daughter. Wells' bitterness is so loud in this passage that it is easy to forget poor Mrs. Wells, who was grieving the sudden loss of her daughter. Reread the passage and get a feel for this mother.

Write a letter of consolation to Mrs. Wells. Have you ever lost someone dear to you? Tell her how God helped you. Include sympathy but no preaching. Think of her heart, not her head.

Dear Bertie

When young Wells—Bertie—was in his formative years, he was affected by his mother's reaction to the sudden death of her only daughter and by his own skepticism. Read the small account below of a piece of his religious history.

> Occasionally I would find myself praying—always to God simply. He remained a God spread all over space and time, yet nevertheless he was capable of special response and magic changes in the order of events. I would pray when I was losing a race, or in trouble in an examination room, or frightened. I expected prompt attention. In my first book-keeping examination by the College of Preceptors I could not get my accounts to balance. I prayed furiously. The bell rang, the invigilator hovered over my last frantic efforts. I desisted reluctantly, "All right, God," I said, "catch me praying again." I was then about twelve.[6]

> Why do people go on pretending about this Christianity? At the test of war, disease, social injustice and every real human distress, it fails—and leaves a cheated victim, as it abandoned my mother . . . . Our Saviour of the Trinity is a dressed-up inconsistent effigy of amiability, a monstrous hybrid of man and infinity, making vague promises of helpful miracles for the cheating of simple souls, an ever absent help in times of trouble.[7]

Wells' last phrase, "an ever absent help in times of trouble," is an allusion to Psalm 46:1 (KJV): "God is our refuge and strength, a very present help in trouble." Write a letter to that young twelve-year-old Bertie who was disillusioned because God did not answer "yes" to his mother's prayers or to his prayers in the classroom. What will you say to him? How will you explain God to him? How can you explain the world's troubles to him so that he will understand their origins?

Teacher, you'll find a grading grid for *The War of the Worlds* on the next page. The grid is marked for a possible 100 points per book. Please feel free to adjust it to your needs and expectations. You have permission to copy it as many times as needed for your own class, co-op, reading group, book-of-the-month club, or family.

56

Grading Grid for *The War of the Worlds*

Student Name: _____

Online "Yes, I read it" quiz, graded online. 1-10 points	
Online literary terms quiz, graded online. 1-10 points	
Participation in opinion questions online. 1-10 points	
Quality of participation in discussions. 1-20 points	
Successful completion of lessons and assignments. 1-20 points	
Successful completion of activity. 1-10 points	
Finished reading the book. 1-20 points.	
Total grade for *The War of the Worlds*	

Chapter 3: *The Friendly Persuasion*

Harcourt, Inc.   ISBN: 0-15-602909-X or 0-15-633606-5

Facebook Posts

If your group or co-op meets monthly, you may want to keep in touch with the students and keep them interested in the novels by creating a secret Facebook group for only them and their parents. Below are the questions I've asked my Facebook group. Feel free to devise your own questions or find your own links to interesting material.

- Here's a link to the trailer for the 1956 movie version of *The Friendly Persuasion*: https://www.youtube.com/watch?v=3BR6dmEhl_Y. Does the trailer make you want to watch the movie?
- Jessamyn West was interviewed by *The Paris Review* in 1977. You can read that fascinating interview by visiting here: http://www.theparisreview.org/interviews/3546/the-art-of-fiction-no-67-jessamyn-west. What surprised you about West or her writing habits?
- In "Shivaree Before Breakfast," we learn of an old custom to celebrate newlyweds. Invent a fresh custom to celebrate new graduates.
- Read this interesting interview with Jessamyn West at http://www.jessamyn.com/jessamyn/jwtalk.html. In there, she talks about what being ill to the point of death did to and for her. If you have been ill, what has it done to or for you? What did you learn from the experience?
- Jessamyn West had a park named after her in Yorba Linda, California, where she grew up. You can view the park through the "eyes" of a DJI Phantom Vision 2 drone here: https://www.youtube.com/watch?v=jk6EQwpvdz8. If you were to have something named after you, what and where would it be?
- In "The Buried Leaf," one of Jess's children finds a hidden treasure buried in the cellar of the old cabin. If you could find a buried treasure, what would you like to find? Tell us about it.
- In "The Battle of Finney's Ford," everyone in the family has a different opinion of what they would do if their home were attacked. What would you do?
- In "The Meeting House," Jess's wen (small, benign tumor) reminds him of his eventual death. In literature terms, it is his *memento mori*. Without being too creepy and depressing about it, what is your *memento mori*?
- On the topic of writing, Jessamyn West says this: "Talent is helpful in writing, but guts are absolutely necessary. Without the guts to try, the talent may never be discovered." What would you like the "guts to try"?
- What question would you like to ask Jessamyn West?

Before You Read the Book

Lesson 1

This Is Different

Teacher, students are learning that *The Friendly Persuasion* is a compilation of short stories originally published in magazines. It does not read as a normal novel would, but it does follow the same main character, Jesse ("Jess") Birdwell and his wife Eliza, both Quakers, through the years. Their children are scattered throughout the stories, too, and we see new ones as the family grows up.

The tensions are low key. Scriptwriters would call many of these plots **education plots**. The *reader* is not educated; the *character* is.

Instead of naming conflicts in *The Friendly Persuasion*, students will identify the tensions or problems. For instance, the two main tensions in the first short story, "Music on the Muscatatuck," might look like this:
1. There is tension between Jesse and his wife because he wants a musical instrument—something Quakers didn't allow—and she is a Quaker minister.
2. Jesse struggles with himself as he goes back and forth between his deep love of music and the Quaker rules against musical instruments.

Suggested Reading and Homework Plan: Preview

Week 1:
- ❑ Complete lessons 1-3.

Week 2: Lesson 4
- ❑ Read the first six chapters of *The Friendly Persuasion* ("Music on the Muscatatuck" through "The Buried Leaf").
- ❑ Answer questions in your Novel Notebook related to each story.
- ❑ Go online to complete the first set of ungraded opinion questions.
- ❑ Optional: Discuss questions from this set of stories. (Lesson 7)

Week 3: Lesson 5
- ❑ Read the last eight chapters of *The Friendly Persuasion* ("A Likely Exchange" through "Homer and the Lilies").
- ❑ Answer questions in your Novel Notebook related to each story.
- ❑ Go online to complete the second set of ungraded opinion questions.
- ❑ Optional: Discuss questions from this set of stories. (Lesson 8)

Week 4:
- ❑ Decide on one activity and begin work on it. You'll find the list of activities at the end of this chapter. **Your teacher will tell you when this is due.**
- ❑ Complete lessons 6-9.

❑ Hand in your activity and relax.

Imitate!

What does a writer do when she has many things to describe in a scene? In *The War of the Worlds*, you learned that H. G. Wells uses specific and vivid verbs to move his refugees along. Here in *The Friendly Persuasion*, Jessamyn West uses a **spatial description** to show readers what the town of Vernon looks like in its chaotic rush to prepare for an attack by Morgan's Raiders. A spatial description uses location. It describes something from left to right, top to bottom, inside to outside, and so forth. It shows readers where everything is by being orderly.

Turn to page 75 ("The Battle at Finney's Ford") in *The Friendly Persuasion* and find the sentence that begins like this: "There were men throwing shovelfuls of earth out of deep holes, preparing to bury silver, money, keepsakes . . . ." Read the rest of that paragraph. What direction does West use when describing the panic of that scene? Write it here: _____. (The answer appears after Meet Jessamyn West.) *She uses a bottom-to-top direction (or low-to-high), beginning with men in deep holes and ending with an old fellow on top of his house.*

You, too, will use a spatial description to describe something of your choice. If you stand in the doorway of your room, for example, you can describe the meaningful elements of your bedroom by going from left to right, floor to ceiling, far wall to door, door to far wall, and so forth. You have many choices when organizing your material in your description.

Write a paragraph describing something you love or can't stand and organize your description spatially. Be sure to incorporate vivid verbs, too, as H. G. Wells does.

Teacher: If you have time in class, you may want to use this as an in-class writing opportunity so students can learn by what their peers have written. If you are teaching a co-op, the paragraph can be due in a week or emailed to you.

Lesson 2

Meet Jessamyn West

Objective: To learn more about this month's author and how her life influenced her stories.

Jessamyn West shares some similarities with Mark Twain and H. G. Wells, and she's related to one of the United States' more notorious presidents, Richard M. Nixon.

Write two things about her life that interest you. *Answers will vary.*

Lesson 3

Literary Terms: Simile and Metaphor

Objective: To learn the terms *simile* and *metaphor* so students can be looking for them as they read and enjoy the pictures they paint.

Teacher, feel free to share other similes or metaphors you've found in *The Friendly Persuasion* or in your own reading.

Literary Terms: Mood and Tone

Objective: To learn the terms *mood* and *tone*.

Your Novel Notebook

Objective: To train students to be observant readers.

Here's what students are recording in their Novel Notebooks, along with page numbers:

- Three similes
- Three metaphors
- Qualities or traits of Jess and Eliza that help them get along and preserve their marriage

Teacher, students will show the first two items on the list to you after they've read the book. They'll refer to the last item (the qualities and traits) during the individual story discussions with you or the class.

To download a FREE Novel Notebook with the questions already in it, go to http://writingwithsharonwatson.com/illuminating-literature-when-worlds-collide-gateway/ .

A Short English Lesson for Thee

Teacher, students are learning how these particular Quakers use "thee" and "thy."

Fun Fact

Students are learning that authors enfold into their stories events and feelings they are most familiar with (the "Write what you know" adage). A list of thirteen things about Jessamyn West's life appears in this section, and students are supposed to find where in *The Friendly Persuasion* she incorporates these real facts from her life. The full list with answers appears in Fun Fact Follow-up after they've read the book.

The Setting and Publication Dates

Objectives:
- To set up the stories for the students so they have an idea of what to expect.
- To see the context in which these stories were written.

Look at the copyright page in *The Friendly Persuasion* and write down the original publication dates (that are the dates of the individual stories)here: <u>1940, 1943, 1944, 1945</u>.

This is the end of Lesson 3.

Suggested Reading and Homework Plan

Week 1:
- ❑ Complete lessons 1-3. If you have not yet finished this week's work, please do so now.

Week 2: Lesson 4
- ❑ Read the first six chapters of *The Friendly Persuasion* ("Music on the Muscatatuck" through "The Buried Leaf").
- ❑ Answer questions in your Novel Notebook related to each story.
- ❑ Go online to complete the first set of ungraded opinion questions.
- ❑ Optional: Discuss questions from this set of stories. (Lesson 7)

Week 3: Lesson 5
- ❑ Read the last eight chapters of *The Friendly Persuasion* ("A Likely Exchange" through "Homer and the Lilies").
- ❑ Answer questions in your Novel Notebook related to each story.
- ❑ Go online to complete the second set of ungraded opinion questions.
- ❑ Optional: Discuss questions from this set of stories. (Lesson 8)

Week 4:
- ❑ Decide on one activity and begin work on it. Thee will find the list of activities at the end of this chapter. **Thy teacher will tell thee when this is due.**
- ❑ Complete lessons 6-9.
- ❑ Hand in thy activity and relax.

Lesson 4

The First Six Chapters

Teacher, this is a week-long lesson. Students are advised to pace themselves.

Students will read the first six chapters of *The Friendly Persuasion*, begin compiling their Novel Notebook lists, and answer a question or two in their Novel Notebook for each story. You may want to collect the notebooks or simply glance at them.

To download a FREE Novel Notebook with the questions already in it, go to http://writingwithsharonwatson.com/illuminating-literature-when-worlds-collide-gateway/ .

At the end of the week, students will go online to answer ungraded opinion questions. The discussion questions for this first half are in lesson 7. However, if your class or reading group would like to discuss them at the end of the first set of stories, feel free to do so.

In the following chapters in this section, an emphasis will be placed on character traits, skills, or abilities that make a marriage run smoothly: "Music on the Muscatatuck," "The Pacing Goose," and "The Battle of Finney's Ford."

You may want to place an over-all emphasis on what people (and students) can do to achieve a long-lasting marriage, as is seen in the pages of *The Friendly Persuasion*.

"Music on the Muscatatuck"

- The tension in this story comes from three separate characters wanting three different things—and these desires conflict with each other. What does Jess want? *Music in the form of an organ. Jess's inner struggle is between his love of music and his Quaker upbringing; his outer struggle is with his wife over the organ.* What does Eliza want? *To stick to the church's rule of no music or musical instruments; to not get into trouble with the visiting Committee and be thrown out of the church.* What does Waldo Quigley want? *To sell Jess an organ.*
- What does Eliza do to help Jess and her get along? *"She had enough respect" for God's ability to reach Jess and respect for Jess "to leave them to each other" (13).*
- What does Jess do to help Eliza and him get along? *He agrees immediately about moving the organ to the attic. For both of them, the ability to compromise, respect each other, see the humor in situations, and so on. Students may have other answers as well.*

"Shivaree before Breakfast"
- There are two separate tensions in this story, and they both involve Josh. What are they? *Josh is angry with and envious of his brother Labe and wishes Labe would be more like him; Josh is repulsed by Old Alf and his version of growing old.*
- On page 27 you read Josh's definition of growing up. Paraphrase it in your own words. *Student's paraphrase should include something about the lack of worry or fear and having everything orderly, happy, and in place.*
- What is your definition of growing up? Use 75 words or fewer. *Student's opinion.*

"The Pacing Goose"
- Astute writers know how to create tension among the characters, and this story is a good example of that. What are Eliza's problems in this story? Jess's? Enoch's? *Eliza's: Someone stole her pet goose, and she decides to go to court to get it back—something Quakers normally didn't do. Jess's: He didn't want Eliza to have geese or go to court. Enoch's: He is stuck in the middle of Jess and Eliza. He wants to obey Jess in the matter of the needle through the eggs, but he is afraid of Eliza and doesn't want her to find out.*

"Lead her like a Pigeon"
- What is Mattie's main problem in this story? *She begins to like Gard but realizes what that might mean someday—leaving her parents—and she's not sure she's ready for everything that means. She may also feel she's being pushed out by her mother or feels the loneliness of walking through that door to marriage by herself (without her mother).*
- Is it resolved by the end of the story? *No. In fact, Jess suggests that it won't be until Mattie has been married for a little while (referring to Eliza's tears shed as a young, lonely bride).*

"The Battle of Finney's Ford"
- What is the main tension in this story? *Josh needs to prove to himself that he is not a coward. By joining the army, he is setting himself against his parents and their religious beliefs.*
- What does Eliza do to show her love to Josh? *Packs food for him.*
- What does Jess do to show his love for Josh? *Gives him a better horse.*
- What character traits help Jess and Eliza get through this difficult time in their lives? *Jess possesses a "kind of calm, a tolerant pliability" (59); he has a great love and regard for Josh (66) and a sense of humor (66); they both find practical things to do for Josh that do not compromise their convictions; they speak honestly and truthfully to him but not harshly or meanly.*

"The Buried Leaf"
1. Mattie has two basic problems in this story. What are they? *She is disenchanted with her father and with her unimaginative place in life.*
2. Write three words to describe Mattie—the kind of girl she is. *A teenage girl, a dreamer, an idealist, slightly self-centered. Her mother comes closest to seeing Mattie clearly.*
3. What does Mattie forgive her father for? *She's an idealist and is disgusted with how he can call the pigs and then eat them later—too commonplace and down-to-earth for her liking. She forgives him for being himself when she hears how adventurous and interesting her relatives had been because this means that she is not stuck here.*

Complete the Online Opinion Survey

Objective: To allow students to express opinions and think about some of the issues in these stories that affect their lives.

Teacher, students will be going to http://writingwithsharonwatson.com/illuminating-literature-when-worlds-collide-gateway/ to get the link to complete ungraded opinion questions on the first six stories in *The Friendly Persuasion.* Students are allowed one attempt for this opinion survey. **Password: JWEST**.

Teacher, if you prefer printed quizzes, you'll find them in *Illuminating Literature: When Worlds Collide, Quiz and Answer Manual,* available for sale at http://writingwithsharonwatson.com/illuminating-literature-when-worlds-collide.

Opinion questions have no correct answer; students are graded on participation. Their answers to the opinion questions may help you develop a strategy for your discussion time.

Lesson 5

The Last Eight Chapters

Teacher, this is a week-long lesson. Students are advised to pace themselves.

Students will read the last eight chapters of *The Friendly Persuasion*, continue compiling their Novel Notebook lists, and answer a question or two in their Novel Notebook for each story. You may want to collect the notebooks or simply glance at them.

To download a FREE Novel Notebook with the questions already in it, go to http://writingwithsharonwatson.com/illuminating-literature-when-worlds-collide-gateway/ .

At the end of the week, students will go online to answer ungraded opinion questions and then discuss as a class the questions pertaining to any stories you want to highlight. The discussion questions are in lesson 8.

In the following chapters in this section, an emphasis will be placed on what character traits, skills, or abilities make a marriage run smoothly: "First Day Finish," "The Vase," and "Pictures from a Clapboard House." Emphasis is also on how to achieve a long-lasting marriage.

"A Likely Exchange"
1. What is Jess's main problem in this story? *He has to find a horse that doesn't look racy to Eliza but that satisfies his need for speed.*
2. What do you think Jess will do with his new horse? *Student opinion.*

"First Day Finish"
The narration mentions "Enoch reading Emerson." Who is Emerson? *Ralph Waldo Emerson*

Jess's quotation at the end of the story is an allusion to an old poem titled "Virtue" by George Herbert. Here's one version of it, from the 1871 hymnal *Hymns for Christian Devotion*:

Sweet day! so cool, so calm, so bright;
Bridal of earth and sky;
The dew shall weep thy fall tonight,
For thou, alas! must die.

Sweet rose! in air whose odors wave,
And color charms the eye;
Thy root is ever in its grave,
And thou, alas! must die.

Sweet spring! of days and roses made,
Whose charms for beauty vie;
Thy days depart, thy roses fade;
Thou, too, alas! must die.

Only a sweet and holy soul
Hath tints that never fly;
White flowers decay and seasons roll,
This lives, and cannot die.

One version of this poem begins the last stanza this way: "Only a sweet and virtuous soul, like seasoned timber, never gives."

1. Here's another story with tensions among a triangle of characters. Name the three characters and the tensions they experience. *Jess and his wife are at odds with each other over the race to meeting; Jess and Reverend Godley each want to win this race; the unseemly race threatens to be grounds to read Jess out of the Meeting.*
2. From the context of the story, guess what being "read out of Meeting" means. *Excommunication.*
3. Read the poem "Virtue" above. How does it apply to "First Day Finish"? *Perhaps Jess is accepting the fact that all earthly things—including horses and horse races—die, but his soul, which is more important to himself, Eliza, and the Meeting, will never die. Perhaps being virtuous means more to him now than racing. Or maybe his race and the after-effects have left him in a good mood, so he thinks of the beautiful day.*

4. In your opinion, which character has the more "virtuous soul": Jess or Eliza? Explain. *Student opinion.*
5. What pulls Jess and Eliza together in this story? *They have a common "enemy" in the Reverend Godley (124); Jess feels regret for his actions because of how they will affect Eliza (125-6); Eliza is eventually "forgiving and gentle" (127); everyday kindnesses of tea, etc. (127).*

"Yes, We'll Gather at the River"
1. What do you think of Lafe Millspaugh? Who do you know that is like him? *Student opinion.*

"The Meeting House"

Teacher, Jessamyn West uses weather here to indicate Jess's changing mood, and students learn a new literary term.

Wen: a tumor or cyst. Little-growth disease or *little-disease*, from which Jasper Rice suffers, is a real disease called Morquio syndrome today. It is a form of dwarfism and can be life-threatening. One of the main characters in Rodman Philbrick's *Freak the Mighty* suffers from this disease, too.

New literature term: **memento mori**. A *memento mori* is an object or work of art that serves as a reminder of death or our mortality and its inevitability. The term is Latin for "Remember that you will die." Examples can be found in architecture, art, death's heads, skulls, the Grim Reaper, and so forth. The skull in act V, scene I in Shakespeare's *Hamlet* serves as a *memento mori* when Hamlet finds the skull of the former court jester who was also a personal friend: "Alas, poor Yorick. I knew him, Horatio: a fellow of infinite jest, of most excellent fancy."

1. At the beginning of this story, before Jess sets out before sunup, how is he feeling and what is the weather? *"One of Jess's bad times...," melancholy, thinking about death and his own mortality, sure that this cyst on his neck was going to kill him (145-7). It was a late spring, frosty and cold (145).*
2. Cite two examples of the changing weather. *Any of the following: Warmer weather, softer wind, trees leafing out, small flowers were opening, dogwoods blooming on his way to Mrs. John Henry Little's (151); sun hung nearer the earth, he took off his coat and felt the heat on his way to Mrs. Rivers' (152).*
3. What is the last indication of spring that seals his mood for him? *Before he could even see them, he smelled the lilies-of-the-valley that had just opened yesterday (160).*
4. What is Jess's *memento mori? The wen.* Do you have something that reminds you of the inevitability of death (without being too creepy about it)? *Answers will vary.*

"The Vase"
Teacher, students learn a new literary term: **symbol.**

The mood of this story is nothing like that of the lighthearted "Yes, We'll Gather at the River," so be forewarned.

The vase and its painted swans in this story, though real objects, are symbols of something else. What's a symbol?

A **symbol** is something that has a meaning on its own, but, when used artfully in a story, can take on another, fuller meaning. In other words, it is something concrete used to show something abstract. A vase is a vase, but it can also *mean* something.
In "The Meeting House," Jess contemplates his own mortality, and his wen is the concrete item that becomes a symbol of his mortality. The wen and his views of it have become a symbol of his mortality.

The tensions here are between husband and wife, for neither can understand the other's point of view. And there's a tension between a happy expectation and the not-so-happy reality.

1. What were the circumstances when Eliza painted the first swan? The second swan? *She painted the first swan in her early marriage; everything was ahead of her and she was eager to meet it. She was full of expectations. She began the second swan soon after her daughter Sarah died, but she never finished it; "It was a miserable day" (168).*
2. Have you ever lost someone dear to you? If so, think of an item that symbolizes that person or pet. *Answers will vary.*
3. Jess and Eliza never do see eye-to-eye in this story. What keeps them together even though they view the world so differently? *Their shared history and grief, their love of their children (both living and dead), Jess's tender heart, Eliza's steadfastness, the idea that they never considered divorce or splitting up as an option, their mutual respect of the other, and so forth.*

"The Illumination"
1. What exactly is the Illumination? *Jess and Eliza are celebrating their new use of gas lighting in their home instead of the coal-oil (kerosene) lamps and candles. They have modernized their house.*
2. What, in your opinion, did Jess mean by "sampling as many of the elements as is possible" (174) and "Eternity is the depth you go"(185)? *Student's opinion, but possibly enjoying life where you can and not stinting yourself on God's good things.* Do you agree with him? *Student's opinion.*
3. Who shows Jess the difference between living life to the full and barely living it? *Old Eli Whitcomb and his miserliness and habit of hoarding.*

68

"Pictures from a Clapboard House"
1. What is Uncle Stephen's pet name for young Elspeth and why does he call her this? *Aunt Jetty (189-90). Her father Gardiner, as you will remember from "Lead her like a Pigeon," is one-quarter American Indian, so we can infer from Stephen's name "Aunt Jetty" that Elspeth has dark-ish skin or hair ("jet" meaning "black").*
2. What secret does Elspeth spill? *She saw Lidy having a picnic with another man last year (190).*
3. Make a prediction: Will Stephen and Lidy's marriage be successful and long-lived? Explain. *Answers will vary.*
4. Do you know someone who married another whom parents did not approve of? How strong is their marriage now? *Answers will vary.*

"Homer and the Lilies"
1. How old is Jess? *Eighty.*
2. How old is Homer? *Twelve.*
3. Why do you think Jess and Homer get along so well? *Jess is lonely and needs someone to love and look after; Homer is lonely and wants someone to care about him. They both share a love of nature and are both "notionate," to borrow a word from "Yes, We'll Gather at the River." They both enjoy talking about their findings and their ideas.*
4. Do you wish you had a Jess in your life? Are you a Jess to someone? *Answers will vary.*

5. Jess considered himself an adult when, at 18 years of age, he "owned a cow and horse and had cleared ten acres" (207). When will you consider yourself an adult? *Answers will vary.*

Complete the Online Opinion Survey

Objective: To allow students to express opinions and think about some of the issues in these stories that affect their lives.

Teacher, students will be going to http://writingwithsharonwatson.com/illuminating-literature-when-worlds-collide-gateway/ to get the link to complete the second set of ungraded opinion questions on the last eight stories in *The Friendly Persuasion.* **Password: JWEST.**

Teacher, if you prefer printed quizzes, you'll find them in *Illuminating Literature: When Worlds Collide, Quiz and Answer Manual,* available for sale at http://writingwithsharonwatson.com/illuminating-literature-when-worlds-collide-gateway/ . Students are allowed one attempt for each opinion survey.

Opinion questions have no correct answer; students are graded on participation. Their answers to the opinion questions may help you develop a strategy for your discussion time.

After Thee Has Read the Book

Lesson 6

Five-Star Report

Teacher, students are circling a number in a chart to indicate how they feel about the book, 1 being "Couldn't stand it" and 5 being "Loved it."

Which stories were thy favorites? Write the titles below and what thee liked about them: *Answers will vary.*

Which stories were thy least favorites? Write the titles below and what thee didn't like about them. *Answers will vary.*

Reward: Distribute the small reward to each student who finished reading *The Friendly Persuasion*. Perhaps cookies, which will tie in to what Mattie brought Gard and his family in "Lead Her Like a Pigeon."

Complete the Online Quizzes

Objectives:
- To complete a short, fact quiz online and a vocabulary quiz in the textbook for grades.
- To reinforce these literary terms: simile, metaphor, mood, tone, allusion, irony, conflict, symbol, and *memento mori*.

Teacher, students are instructed to go to http://WritingWithSharonWatson.com/illuminating-literature-when-worlds-collide-gateway/ to get links to complete the following:
- "Yes, I read it" quiz—graded online for you
- Literary Terms Quiz (simile, metaphor, mood, tone, allusion, irony, conflict, symbol, and *memento mori*)—graded online for you

Password for quizzes for *The Friendly Persuasion*: JWEST.

Teacher, if you prefer printed quizzes, you'll find them in *Illuminating Literature: When Worlds Collide, Quiz and Answer Manual*, available for sale at http://writingwithsharonwatson.com/illuminating-literature-when-worlds-collide-gateway/ .

Teacher, students are allowed two attempts for the "Yes, I read it" quiz and the literary terms quiz. Also, the quiz site will email a full report of the quiz (questions, your student's answers, the correct answers, and your student's grade) to the email address your student signed in with.

Vocabulary Quizzola for *The Friendly Persuasion*

Objectives:
- To reinforce good vocabulary habits and awareness.
- To gain a grade, which is separate from the Grading Grid.

Directions: Match the definition on the right with the correct word on the left by entering the letter in the correct blank. The page numbers in parentheses are where the word can be found in the Harcourt, Brace & Company or the Harcourt, Inc. version of *The Friendly Persuasion*. **Ask your teacher if this is an open-book quiz.**

D__1. Dido (4)
J__2. Scions (29)
F__3. Burgeoning (29)
M__4. Pie plant (31)
G__5. Convexity (36)
B__6. Vexed (36)
I__7. Amicable (38)
C__8. Terse (42)
O__9. Truculence (42)
L__10. Bosky (54)
S__11. Verity (119)
T__12. Restive (126)
N__13. Notionate (138)
P__14. Picayunish (146)
Q__15. Asperity (160)
U__16. Gilded (164)
A__17. Jet (189)
K__18. Stolid (208)
E__19. Lucidity (212)
R__20. First Day (15)
H__21. Shivaree (18)

A. black
B. irked, bothered
C. concise or brief
D. fancy but useless frill
E. clearness of thinking
F. sprouting, beginning to grow
G. roundness
H. an impromptu party for newlyweds
I. friendly
J. human or horticultural descendants
K. not easily excited
L. wooded or bushy
M. rhubarb
N. full of ideas
O. aggressiveness
P. small, petty
Q. sharp temper
R. Sunday
S. truth
T. fidgety
U. of a gold color or painted or colored gold

Total number correct: _____
Vertical word encoded out in your correct answers: <u>QUAKER</u>

Correct answers are worth 5 points each (or 4.8 points, if you want to get technical).

Lesson 7

Questions for Discussion 1

Objectives:
- To discuss important topics touched on in *The Friendly Persuasion*.
- To discuss and understand what it takes to have a happy, healthy, long-lasting marriage.

Teacher, ask students these questions to get the ball rolling:

1. What questions do you have about these stories?
2. What aspects of this book appealed to you?
3. Which story is your favorite one?

These preliminary questions will help to clear up any misunderstandings or miscomprehensions from the stories, and they'll get students talking during the discussion session. Students can answer other students' questions, too. This pre-discussion time may also serve to answer some of the questions printed below or can be a springboard to any of the aspects of the book you want to focus on.

Please choose the questions that are most appropriate for your class, your time, and the students' interests.

Students have answered some of these questions in their Novel Notebooks already. They may want to refer to the notebooks during the discussion.

Discussion questions for "Music on the Muscatatuck"
1. What kind of man is Jess? Cite examples. *A feeling man who appreciates nature and all he's been given (4); "pined for music"(4); sociable (5); heart as soft as pudding (12) unless commanded (12); no hypocrite (16); conscious of sin and quick to repent (16); can't hold him back where his heart is concerned (17).*
2. How is the idyllic setting in the opening of this story different from the one of Dawson's Landing in *Pudd'nhead Wilson*? *One is rural, the other is in town. The setting in* Pudd'nhead Wilson *is used to show the irony between the setting and the citizens' hearts; the setting in "Music on the Muscatatuck" is used to set the book in its proper place, to set a positive mood, and to showcase its owner, Jess. No irony. No negative or hidden message.*
3. Do you like Jess? Why or why not? *Student opinion.*
4. Would you like to belong to this family? Why or why not? *Student opinion*
5. There is something ironic in what Amos Pease says to Jess. What is it? *Although Quakers were not supposed to use musical instruments, Amos Pease declares that Jess has been an instrument: "thee's been an instrument of the Lord this night" (16).*
6. How do you decide whether a conviction is worth holding on to? *Student opinion.*
7. Do you have any personal convictions that are as pliable as Jess's? *Student opinion.*
8. What things are so integral to my walk with God that I cannot compromise on them? *Student opinion*
9. In your opinion, what would have happened next if Eliza had stayed out in the snow or had not compromised? *Student opinion.*
10. What character traits or qualities do Jess and Eliza exhibit that help them get along with each other? *The ability to compromise, respect each other, see the*

humor in situations, and so on. Jess agrees immediately about moving the organ to the attic. "She [Eliza] had enough respect" for God's ability to reach Jess and for Jess "to leave them to each other" (13). Students may have other answers as well.

Discussion questions for "Shivaree before Breakfast"
1. Who is older, Labe or Josh? *Josh is 13; Labe is 10.*
2. What were Josh's physical and mental reactions to Old Alf and his bride? *Stared, backed toward the door, spoke with a dry voice, felt cold, heart like lead, called Old Alf crazy, flat against the kitchen door, fear in his eyes, disgusted, afraid (26-7).*
3. What were Labe's physical and mental reactions to Old Alf and his bride? *Stared, backed toward the door, smiled, asked an interested question, moved closer to Alf, hated to go, accepted an offer to come again, intrigued (26-8)*
4. Which boy's reactions seem right to you? *Student's opinion.*

Discussion questions for "The Pacing Goose"
1. Is Enoch Quaker? How do you know? *No, he doesn't use* thee *and* thy.
2. List the three things Jess learned at the trial. *1. Dependability is a woman's greatest virtue. 2. In the case of a woman versus the law, the woman will win. 3. Never hire a hired man until you know he can count to eight.*

Discussion questions for "Lead her like a Pigeon"
1. To what does Jud Bent compare Mattie? *Spring.*
2. What is the song about on page 52? *Falling in love and getting married.*
3. Who are Persephone and Pluto? What does Jud Bent mean by saying, "Don't eat any pomegranate seeds"? *In Greek mythology, Persephone was the daughter of an earth goddess and possibly the goddess of spring. Pluto (or Hades) was the god of the Underworld. When Pluto lured Persephone into his world, he tricked her into eating some pomegranate seeds, sacred to the Underworld. She was doomed to live underground for three months every year; therefore, we have good weather for nine months (when Persephone is above ground) and three months of cold weather (when Persephone is in the Underworld). Basically, Jud was making a joke about his son and Mattie liking each other.*
4. Why did Mattie suddenly cry? *She realized that by growing up, falling in love, and marrying, she would have to leave her house and her parents. She wasn't quite ready to do that and felt that her mother was pushing her out.*

Discussion questions for "The Battle of Finney's Ford"
1. In your opinion, which do you think is right about death and curses, Josh or Jess? *Student opinion.*
2. Is Josh disappointed with his experience? *In what happened to him, yes: "This is war. It's falling over a cliff, cracking thy skull and puking" (88). In going, no. He had faced his fear (91).*

3. How does Labe know to look for Josh? *The horse Rome had returned home (89).*
4. Why does Josh decide he has to fight? *Because he hates it (89). He needs to prove to himself that he isn't a coward.*
5. Why does Labe decide he shouldn't fight? *Because he likes it (89).*
6. What is your opinion of fighting in a war? *Student opinion*
7. How does Josh get hurt? *He falls over a cliff in the dark and is knocked out(87).*
8. How long is Josh gone at war? *About 24 hours (90).*
9. Is Josh disappointed in himself? *No, he has faced his fear (91).*
10. In "Music on the Muscatatuck," Jess breaks a church rule and buys a musical instrument. In "The Battle of Finney's Ford," Josh breaks a church rule and goes to war. Are there any differences in the rule breaking? If so, how are they different? *Answers will vary.*
11. What character traits or qualities do Jess and Eliza exhibit that help them get along with each other during this difficult time in their lives? *Mutual support, kindness, and so forth. Jess possesses a "kind of calm, a tolerant pliability" (59); he has a great love and regard for Josh (66) and a sense of humor (66); they both find practical things to do for Josh that do not compromise their convictions; they speak honestly and truthfully to him but not harshly or meanly.*

Discussion questions for "The Buried Leaf"
1. Why does Little Jess want to dig in the open cellar of the old house? *He had a dream (94).*
2. What do Mattie and Little Jess find? *A buried box in the cellar of the old house (96).*
3. What does she forgive her father for? *She's an idealist and is disgusted with how he can call the pigs and then eat them later—too commonplace and down-to-earth for her liking. She forgives him for being himself when she hears how adventurous and interesting her relatives had been because this means that she is not stuck here.*
4. How long had it been buried? *50 years (98).*
5. Find the Bible reference for the verses Jess reads. *Deuteronomy 26: 8-9, 15 (101).*
6. Would you like to belong to this family? Why or why not? *Student opinion.*

Lesson 8

Questions for Discussion 2

Objectives:
- To discuss important topics touched on in *The Friendly Persuasion*.
- To discuss and understand what it takes to have a happy, healthy, long-lasting marriage.

Teacher, ask students these questions to get them talking:

1. What questions do you have about these stories?
2. What aspects of this book appealed to you?
3. What are some common threads that tie these stories together?

These preliminary questions will help to clear up any misunderstandings or miscomprehensions from the stories, and they'll get students talking during the discussion session. Students can answer other students' questions, too. This pre-discussion time may also serve to answer some of the questions printed below or can be a springboard to any of the aspects of the book you want to focus on.

Please choose the questions that are most appropriate for your class, your time, and the students' interests.

Students have answered some of these questions in their Novel Notebooks already. They may want to refer to them during the discussion.

Discussion questions for "A Likely Exchange"
1. What do Jess's customers think of him? Are they right? *A good man, notional, a Quaker, a plain-speaker (108).*
2. What lesson does Jess learn on this trip to Kentucky? *Not to judge by appearance (112).*
3. Do you think a slower horse will help Opal, Ruby, Pearl, and Bertha find husbands? *Student opinion*
4. What cars today are analogous to Red Rover, that looks racy but isn't, and Lady, that looks like a clunker but is wonderfully fast? *Student opinion*

Discussion questions for "First Day Finish"
1. *We see how the Meeting reacts to the race. How do you think the Reverend Godley's congregation reacted? *Student opinion*
2. What pulls Jess and Eliza together in this story? *They have a common "enemy" in the Reverend Godley (124); Jess feels regret for his actions because of how they will affect Eliza (125-6); Eliza is eventually "forgiving and gentle" (127); everyday kindnesses of tea, etc. (127).*
3. What are "eternal verities"? *Eternal truths*

Discussion question for "Yes, We'll Gather at the River"
1. It's hard to imagine a time when a room dedicated to bathing was unusual, but now we can't do without it. What today can't you imagine being without? *Student opinion*

Discussion questions for "The Meeting House"
1. As a lad, Jess had thought that "The Lord is my shepherd, I shall not want" was really "The shepherd I shall not want." Tell of a time when your younger self mixed up a saying, religious or otherwise. *Answers will vary.*

2. Of the three customers, which one did the most to wake him out of his mood? Why this particular one? *The sickly Mrs. Rivers because he compares his troubles to hers and realizes she has more to lose and is worse off than he is. In addition, he helps her, which takes the emphasis off himself. Also, he sees how she is marching on despite her troubles and is not filled with self-pity.*

3. What is ironic in this story? *Jess is a godly man who stays the night in a married woman's house so he can do things for her she can't do by herself. Meanwhile, the one who should be doing things for her—her husband—is off with another woman. Jess's sleeping situation seems like that of the husband but is far from it.*

4. Why doesn't Jess stop at the Fair Hope Meeting House as he had planned? *He is no longer feeling melancholy or ready to die, and he explains that "boards don't make the only meeting houses" as he thumps his chest (160). "Here's a spot too, for praying and learning." God had spoken to his heart as Jess traveled and visited. His heart is the Meeting House.*

Discussion questions for "The Vase"

1. How does Jess view his wife's artwork? *He barely sees it, is mostly unaware of it, and doesn't value it.*

2. How does Eliza view her husband's love of nature? *She doesn't understand it, thinks it wasteful of his time, thinks he is making the wrong things important.*

3. Who is right: Jess or Eliza? *Answers will vary, most likely depending on individual student experiences, learning styles, and preferences.*

4. When Jess hugs Eliza, and the vase is between them, what is this action telling the reader? *Neither of them sees eye-to-eye about some important things in their lives, but they are linked together by their lives and their sorrows and Sarah's death.*

5. What are the vase and the swans symbols of? *The first swan, fully rendered, is a symbol of Eliza's expectations for her life with Jess—family, children, happy days ahead. The second swan, only in outline, is a symbol of the stark reality of Sarah's death, which is even worse than an unfulfilled expectation.*

6. Jess and Eliza never do see eye-to-eye in this story. What keeps them together? *It is true that there is a higher likelihood of a marriage breaking up after the death of a child, so this question bears looking into. Some possible answers: their mutual love for each other despite their differing views, their full life history of successfully living together, Jess' tender heart, Eliza's steadfastness, and the fact that neither of them ever contemplated divorce.*

Discussion questions for "The Illumination"

1. Have you ever insulted someone unintentionally, like Jess does to his daughter Jane? *Answers will vary.*

2. What is the concrete event of the Illumination a symbol of? In other words, what else is being "illuminated"? *The Illumination is a symbol of the light shed in Jess's heart when he realizes just how good his life is, even though his neighbor believes Jess is pouring his money "down the drainpipe" (184). It*

shows Jess that his generosity throughout his life has been the right thing to do instead of hoarding things, as he tells Eli, "I never figured it in that light."

Discussion questions for "Pictures from a Clapboard House"
1. Name two reasons why Jess and Eliza regret Stephen's choice of a wife. *She is a non-Quaker, and they believe her to have been unfaithful with Mel Venters on some level when she was engaged to Stephen.*
2. Does Stephen seem troubled by the secret? *He already knew it; by the end of the story, he "looked buoyant and well, serene and happy" (198).* By his parents' opinion of Lidy? *Yes, enough to burst into their bedroom unannounced (198). That was probably the first and only time he did that.*
3. What do you think Lidy wrote in her note to Mel Venters? *Student opinion. The scene on the balcony at the shivaree seems to indicate that she wrote a good-bye note.*
4. Do you believe Stephen when he tells his parents why he loves Lidy? *Student opinion.*
5. Make a prediction: Will Stephen and Lidy's marriage be successful and long-lived? *Answers will vary.*
6. Do you know someone who married another whom parents did not approve of? How strong is their marriage now? *Answers will vary.*

Discussion questions for "Homer and the Lilies"
1. Why do you think Jess likes Homer so much? *He sees something of himself in Homer.*
2. Jess considered himself an adult when, at 18 years old, he "owned a cow and horse and had cleared ten acres" (207). When will you consider yourself an adult? *Student opinion.*
3. Explain the difference between doing people good and loving your fellow man as Jess sees the difference. *Student's opinion.*
4. Is there a difference to you? Explain. Which would you rather do? *Student's opinion.*
5. Jess and Eliza wondered if they were spoiling Homer. What constitutes spoiling a child? *Student opinion*

Two culturally relevant questions on the topic of marriage:
1. Kurt Braunohler, speaking on the radio program *This American Life*, says of himself and his former girlfriend, "We both had this kind of arrogant notion of our relationship, that it could survive literally anything."[8] Jess and Eliza's marriage survived a child's death, war, separation, disappointment with each other and with children's choices, inability to understand the other's views, and many other hardships. Why is the axis of arrogance and humility not a helpful basis from which to have a discussion on longevity in marriage? *It implies that if you are going into a marriage to make it last, if that is your goal, that you are arrogant.* What is the secret of their marriage's ability to "survive literally anything"? *Mutual respect, a sense of humor, unselfishness, working hard to make sure the other person is taken care of, not giving the idea*

of divorce a thought, appreciating the sense of achievement and history built up over the years, they accommodate each other in matters that are not moral or ethical in nature, and so forth. Were they arrogant, or is their success attributed to something else? *The argument is not balanced on the terms "arrogant" or "humble." It centers on each partner's expectations for a long-lasting marriage, how they will achieve it, what they will do to build a healthy relationship and avoid separation or divorce, determination to provide a safe and healthy environment for their children, and choosing to love their spouse on bad days and through horrible events.* How can a long-lasting marriage be achieved today? *Answers will vary.*

2. In the same radio program, Braunohler reveals that he and his live-in girlfriend "had known each other our whole adult lives. We were each other's world, so really, I don't think we thought that we could destroy this thing." What do people do today that can destroy their marriages? *Answers will vary.*

Lesson 9

Your Novel Notebook Follow-up

1. Three similes. *A partial list:*
    - *It's like a ship...(19)*
    - *...like a hornet, ready to sting (19)*
    - *...like a snake on stilts (33)*
    - *...like a slack sail...(36)*
    - *...like a burning timber (78)*
    - *...wizened up like a cabbage leaf under a hot sun (111).*
    - *He stood there...holding the eggs in front of him like some kind of scraggy limb, fallen from a tree with nest attached (130).*
    - *...as merry as a wedding bell and noisy as a foundry (140).*
    - *...like the clapper in the middle of a sounding bell (161).*
    - *...stand thus at the day's rim as over a pool of water before plunging in (174).*
    - *...as silent and at peace as the clapper in a ropeless bell (174).*
    - *They darted like needles through the morning...(178)*
    - *...her cold bed which stood anchored like a little boat at the foot of grandma's great full-sailed four-poster bed (190).*
2. Three metaphors. *A partial list:*
    - *. . . carried us all upwards on thy pinions . . . (17)*
    - *...a dragon-fly ran its darning needle...(80)*
    - *...he didn't plan always to move up the pike a tail to Godley's comet (106).*
    - *...instead of the corn, that great surge of water and the boats it bore: white-pillared swans, floating verandas (108).*
    - *Eliza grabbed at a straw in the passing flood (138). [This one is appropriate as they are talking about water and the bathtub.]*

- *...they wove the bright May morning into a fabric strong enough to support a party...Jane and Jess feather-stitched around the edges (178).*
- *The balloon of party preparations...(181).*

3. Qualities or traits of Jess and Eliza that help them get along and preserve their marriage. *These have been covered in the discussions of the individual stories.*

Fun Fact Follow-up

Teacher, students will be showing you the page numbers where they found these parts of Jessamyn West's life scattered throughout these stories.

1. Jessamyn's mother's family took an orphan boy from Indianapolis into their home. They fed and clothed him, and he did chores for them. <u>200-2</u>
2. They also kept a starling in a cage on the porch. <u>3</u>
3. Grace (Jessamyn's mother) met her future husband at his aunt's house nearby. He was visiting. Grace rode barefoot and bareback to deliver cookies her mother had baked. <u>49-50</u>
4. Eldo, Jessamyn's father, had Comanche blood in him <u>70,</u> and his mother was biracial—half American Indian. <u>47</u>
5. As a child, Grace wished she had been named Gladys because it sounded more exotic. <u>92-3</u>
6. Jessamyn described her mother making pies with a "birdlike flutter of her hands." <u>172</u>
7. She described her grandpa (Jesse Milhous) as a good man who, by conviction, had never tasted alcohol. <u>9</u>
8. Grace liked to hear her mother's wedding ring click against the glasses she was washing. <u>53</u>
9. Grace told Jessamyn of an old man she had known who had made up a wife to talk to when he thought he was alone. <u>23-6</u>
10. Jessamyn liked to go outside her house and look in through the windows from a distance. <u>183</u>
11. Her grandmother hand painted scenes of cattails and swans on her footstools. <u>48, 163</u>
12. This same woman was small, had black hair, and was a hard worker. <u>3</u>
13. Jessamyn had a kitten while she was recovering from tuberculosis at her mother's house. It would sleep under the covers at her feet. <u>157</u>

The Double Meaning

1. *Quakers today are often called Friends. The word* persuasion *can be used for a person's religious belief: "He is of the Methodist persuasion." Thus, you have the literal meaning of the title.*
2. *The second meaning is, of course, trying to make someone see things your way (persuade them) but being amiable and kind (friendly) about it, much as Eliza demonstrates in the courtroom with the young judge in "The Pacing Goose." Jess often uses a friendly persuasion when he is planning on doing something Eliza may not like, such as constructing a room in the house for a bathtub.*

In this novel, who is persuaded in a friendly manner? *Answers will vary.*

Except for Me and Thee

Students are learning about a companion novel to *The Friendly Persuasion* titled *Except for Me and Thee*. It, too, follows Jess Birdwell through the years, filling in gaps left in the first book.

If You Liked This Book . . .

Students are viewing a list of books similar in theme or tone to *The Friendly Persuasion*.

What other books would you like to add to this list? *Student opinion*

This is the end of lesson 9.

Your Choice of Activities

Note: Choose only one of the following activities. Read all of them carefully before you make your decision. Below you will find a short explanation of each activity. **Your teacher will tell you when this is due.**

> List Mania – Compile a collection of quotations.
> An Un-Quaker Song – Play, sing, or write a song.
> I'll Watch the Movie – Compare book to movie and give a movie review.
> The Naturalist—Give a nature presentation or tour
> You're the Chef – Cook dishes found in the book.
> Tea Time – Brew sassafras tea.
> Hello, Me – Write a letter to the younger Jessamyn West.
> More Lasting Than . . . – Finish "Love is more lasting than…."
> Treasure or Weather – Write a short story or an alternate ending.
> History Buff – Research Quaker history and beliefs.

The activities are explained below.

List Mania

Jessamyn West kept many lists and journals. One list included the names of the winds and their descriptions because she loved the wind in all its forms. In a separate journal, she kept quotations on the subject of pity. Anytime she came across an interesting quotation about pity, she wrote it in what she called her pity anthology.

You, too, can start a list or an anthology—a collection—of your own. Choose a subject that interests you and begin to collect quotations from other authors on this subject. And—unlike Jess, who put false names to his quotations in "The Illumination"—get the author's name right!

An Un-Quaker Song

Many songs are either sung or alluded to in *The Friendly Persuasion*. Examine old songbooks in the library or in used bookstores to find one of those songs. Learn to sing it or play it on a musical instrument before an interested audience. Or write your own song based on something you read in the book. Then perform it before an interested audience.

I'll Watch the Movie

Find the movie version of *The Friendly Persuasion* and watch it. Although the book's timeline was 40 years, the movie takes place during a Civil War summer in order to capitalize on the conflict between war and Quaker pacifism.

Be aware of the differences between the book and the movie, both written by Jessamyn West. Write a movie review for it as though it just came out this year.

The Naturalist

Did you resonate with Jess when he was listening to the rain in "The Vase"? Did you find his conversations with young Homer interesting in "Homer and the Lilies"? Are you intrigued with Jess's vocation with berry plants and trees?

Prepare a presentation on something that you love that is nature related and present it to your class or reading group. Think outside the classroom, if possible. For instance, if you know a lot about spring vegetation, forests, waterfalls, desert life, or bogs, see if you can arrange to be a tour guide to one of these places for your group or class.

You're the Chef

Certain foods are mentioned in *The Friendly Persuasion*. Choose a few and cook or bake them for a class or for your family. If you're really brave, you might choose to cook the food item in the same way Eliza would have cooked her meals—on a wood-burning cook stove or over a fire.

Tea Time

Sassafras tea is mentioned in "The Pacing Goose." Buy some sassafras tea concentrate or some ground-up sassafras root. Learn where it comes from, its health benefits, and its dangers. Brew it, drink it, and decide if you like it.

Hello, Me

You will remember from reading Meet Jessamyn West that she suffered from undiagnosed tuberculosis (TB) symptoms for two years, was in the terminal ward of a TB sanatorium for two years and was sent home to die. For a total of 15 years, she fought this life-threatening disease of the lungs.

Feverish, she lay flat on her back in the sanatorium with a ten-pound bag of buckshot on her chest, languishing away to unhealthy thinness, and listening to the coughs and blood-soaked spit-ups of her fellow sufferers. Jessamyn received little hope from the doctors or nurses about a recovery, and every morning she watched the hearse drive away with yet another inmate who hadn't made it. She contemplated suicide.

This is what she later wrote about those days: "I longed to die and have it over with, and wept each morning to find that I was, alas, still alive. Alive, but without any life to live. I had no future."[9]

You know from reading about Mark Twain in the chapter on *Pudd'nhead Wilson* that he was at his lowest ebb and was contemplating suicide at the same moment that his first short story, "The Celebrated Jumping Frog of Calaveras County," was becoming a big hit in the East. Jessamyn West, too, thought she had no future as each day stretched out unendingly like the day before it, yet she became a successful writer, teacher, and surrogate mother.

In this activity, you are to pretend that you are an older version of Jessamyn West. Write a letter to her younger self to encourage her in her daily near-death struggles. What wisdom from your older self will you share with your younger self?

More Lasting Than . . .

In "Pictures from a Clapboard House," you hear Stephen say, "Love is more lasting than . . ." before his voice is lost on the staircase. Elspeth repeats the phrase the next morning, mulling it over.

How would you finish that phrase? Love is more lasting than—what? Determine the ending, and then write a poem, song, short story, or short essay to show what love is more lasting than.

Treasure or Weather

Did you like what Little Jess dug up in "The Buried Leaf"? Were you satisfied with Mattie's reaction to the treasure? Write another ending to that story. Imagine that something else was dug up and unearthed. What would it be? How would it affect Mattie and her family?

Or use your new tool of creating or highlighting the mood of a story by the use of weather. Remember how Jessamyn West used that writer's device in "The Meeting House"? Write a short story in which someone changes from beginning to end; use the weather to signal to the reader what changes are going on in the character's mind, heart, or circumstances.

History Buff

Quakers have been around for a few hundred years. Where did they come from? Who began the movement? Who were the major players? Was it essentially a religious or a political movement? What were the tenets of their beliefs that made them different from other people groups? Learn why their early husbands and wives weren't really married and who their strongest antagonist was. Find out about modern Quakers (Society of Friends), too.

Research this interesting group of people and write a report on them.

Teacher, you'll find a grading grid for *The Friendly Persuasion* on the next page. The grid is marked for a possible 100 points per book. Please feel free to adjust it to your needs and expectations. You have permission to copy it as many times as needed for your own class, co-op, reading group, book-of-the-month club, or family.

Grading Grid for *The Friendly Persuasion*

Student Name: _____

Online "Yes, I read it" quiz, graded online. 1-10 points	
Online literary terms quiz, graded online. 1-10 points	
Participation in opinion questions online. 1-10 points	
Quality of participation in discussions. 1-20 points	
Successful completion of lessons and assignments. 1-20 points	
Successful completion of activity. 1-10 points	
Finished reading the book. 1-20 points.	
Total grade for *The Friendly Persuasion*	

Writing with
Sharon Watson

84

Chapter 4: *Peter Pan*

Dover Publications   ISBN: 0-486-40783-7

Facebook Posts

- Watch this video and tell us what you learned about J. M. Barrie that interests you: https://www.youtube.com/watch?v=CcR4_yytYNA
- "Manolescent" (as opposed to an "adolescent") is a "man of any age who shirks adult responsibilities," according to the Urban Dictionary. In your opinion, how can teens become adults who take care of their responsibilities and know the consequences of their actions?
- Is it true that if you endure pain and hardships, they will make you a man? Watch this National Geographic video "Initiation with Ants." And tell us what you think: https://www.youtube.com/watch?v=ZGIZ-zUvotM
- If you were to devise a ritual or celebration for becoming an adult, what would it be?
- I love it when we get to hear famous authors in their own voices. Here's a short audio clip of Barrie speaking before an audience and remembering an accident he had with a friend of his in their youth. Enjoy his Scottish burr: http://www.jmbarrie.co.uk/view/7078/.
- James Barrie commissioned this statue to stand in Kensington Gardens, where he originally met the Davies brothers. If you were to commission a statue or other work of art, what would it be? If you were to create a statue or other work of art for someone else, what would it be? http://golondon.about.com/od/londonforfree/ss/Peter_Pan.htm#step-heading
- Are you looking forward to becoming an adult? Tell us about it.
- In honor of Wendy and Mrs. Darling, let's talk about mothers. What is there about your mother that is better than other mothers?
- Barrie used to write little notes in tiny writing and leave them in hollow trees for the Davies brothers to find. If you were to write a little fairy note to someone, to whom would it be addressed and what would it say?
- If Peter Pan had asked you to go, would you have? https://www.youtube.com/watch?v=0ikvTYmANp4
- What question would you like to ask James Barrie?

Before You Read the Book

Lesson 1

Suggested Reading and Homework Plan: Preview

Week 1:
- ❑ Complete lessons 1-4.

Week 2:
   ❏ Read the first eight chapters of *Peter Pan* ("Peter Breaks Through" – "The Mermaids' Lagoon").
Week 3:
   ❏ Read the last nine chapters of *Peter Pan* ("The Never Bird" – "When Wendy Grew Up").
Week 4:
   ❏ Rejoice! There is no activity this month!
   ❏ Complete lessons 5-8.

Imitate!

Read pages 43-49 ("The Island Come True") in *Peter Pan* and notice that when Barrie introduces the lost boys, pirates, and Indians to us, he drops into present tense: "The first to pass is Tootles . . . and he passes by, biting his knuckles." We even see the lost boys killing a pirate in present tense. But when he gets to Captain Hook, between the pirates and the Indians, he uses the past tense.

These narrative shifts in the form of tense changes accentuate the characters and the action. We can feel ourselves dropping down behind a bush on our hands and knees as each lost boy passes in front of us.

Choose a page or so from another book and change the tense. If the author uses the past tense, use the present. If the author uses the present tense, switch it to the past. Then decide which version you like better and explain why.

Teacher: If you have time in class, you may want to use this as an in-class writing opportunity so students can learn by what their peers have written. If you are teaching a co-op, the paragraph can be due in a week or emailed to you.

Lesson 2

Meet Sir Barrie

Now it's time to meet the man who stated in his mother's biography, "Nothing that happens after we are twelve matters very much."

This month you are helping to compile Barrie's biography. Research James Matthew Barrie and fill in the blanks below.

- James Matthew Barrie was born in Kirriemuir, <u>Scotland</u>, in the year <u>1860</u>.
- He was called "<u>Jamie</u>" as a young boy.
- When Barrie was six years old, his older brother <u>David</u> died in an <u>ice-skating</u> accident. His mother was so torn apart by this that she refused to believe he was really dead; in fact, she began calling little Jamie by his brother's name, to which he would answer. He even dressed and whistled like David had, just to try to

make his mother happy. Little Jamie even kept track of how many times he'd made his mother laugh so he could show the doctor. Jamie became so adept at mimicking others' speech and mannerisms that he attended a funeral in place of a friend so his friend didn't have to go, and he pulled it off so well that no one noticed the substitution.

- In school, Jamie was an ardent reader and even helped to form a <u>drama</u> club.
- He was very (circle one): exuberant moody <u>shy</u> angry.
- After attending the University of Edinburgh, he found a job as an anonymous feature writer for the *Nottingham Journal*. His job was to write an article on whatever topic his editor assigned: my umbrella, roses, and so forth. He studied how former articles of this sort were written and then started writing his own— five days a week.
- In a case of "write what you know," Barrie wrote a series of articles based on his grandfather's religious sect called Auld Licht ("Old Light"), as told to him by his mother, who had grown up in it. Is this beginning to sound a lot like Jessamyn West writing about her mother's parents in *The Friendly Persuasion*? Anyway, these articles were popular and were eventually gathered together into three books: *Auld Licht Idylls* (1888), *A Window in Thrums* (1890), and *The Little Minister* (1891).
- Barrie's father was a <u>weaver</u>, so it was very natural for Barrie to change the name of his hometown in *A Window in Thrums* from Kirriemuir to Thrums, a term from his father's profession. Robert Louis Stevenson loved *The Little Minister* so much that, in a letter to Barrie, Stevenson admitted that he personally was a "capable artist" but that Barrie was "a man of genius." Barrie compared writing to his father's occupation.
- He founded a <u>cricket</u> team dubbed the Allahakbarries in his honor. The name is taken from the Arabic *Allah Akbar* ("God help us"). Other authors who enjoyed playing on the Allahakbarries were A. A. Milne (Winnie-the-Pooh stories), Arthur Conan Doyle (of Sherlock Holmes fame), Jerome K. Jerome (*Three Men in a Boat*), and P. G. Wodehouse (creator of that infamous pair Wooster and Jeeves). During World War I, he also formed relationships with playwright George Bernard Shaw and essayist G. K. Chesterton.
- He married the actress <u>Mary Ansell</u> in 1894. It was an unhappy marriage that ended in divorce about fifteen years later.
- Barrie was not tall. In fact, his 1934 passport puts him at <u>5' 3 ½"</u>, which might have been an exaggeration. When he traveled to America, one newspaper described him as being about 125 pounds and having pale cheeks, a big head, and a prominent nose and forehead.
- He had a lifetime cough, left over from a major bout with pneumonia.
- 1897 was an important year for Barrie because that is when he met the <u>Davies</u> boys George, Jack (John), and baby Peter in <u>Kensington Gardens</u>. A few years later, Michael and then Nicholas (Nico) were born. He delighted them all by wiggling his ears; having adventures with them in the park; and leaving tiny

- notes written in small, "fairy" handwriting and hidden in hollow trees. Based on the popularity of his play *The Little White Bird*, which featured Peter Pan as a baby, Barrie was presented with a private, working key to Kensington Gardens.
- The boys' mother <u>Sylvia</u> seemed to enjoy this intruder in their lives; their father <u>Arthur</u> did not. The boys called Barrie "<u>Uncle Jim</u>," as did the many nieces, nephews, and children of associates he loved to hang out with.
- Soon after the Barries bought a cottage on Black Lake forty miles south of London, the Davies family rented a house there as well. Summers were filled with pirates, fairies, crocodiles, and cunning mermaids.
- Barrie wrote many plays before he wrote the play *Peter Pan*, which was first performed just after Christmas in the year <u>1904</u>. The original draft of *Peter Pan* did not include Captain Hook. Peter was to be the villain!
- Mr. and Mrs. Davies were in attendance on opening night. Barrie was a bundle of nerves; what if the audience didn't clap to "resurrect" <u>Tinker Bell</u>? He needn't have worried. *Peter Pan: Or the Boy who Would not Grow Up* was an instant success.
- Mark Twain saw *Peter Pan* in America and liked it.
- At the urging of his friends, Barrie wrote the play into book form in the year <u>1928</u>.
- Barrie's adventures with the Davies boys became Peter Pan's adventures; Mrs. Darling was modeled after Sylvia Davies, the boys' mother; Wendy was modeled after Barrie's mother; Nana was based upon Barrie's dogs Porthos and Luath; and James Hook owes his existence to James M. Barrie, who played the part of Hook in the Kensington Garden and Black Lake adventures.
- Arthur Davies developed <u>cancer</u>. Barrie paid all his hospital and medical expenses. Davies died in 1907.
- Three years later, Sylvia Davies died of <u>cancer</u> as well.
- Barrie took the Davies boys under his wing and became their guardian.
- When Barrie was named a literary baronet—Sir James M. Barrie, Bart ("Bart" is short for "baronet." Who knew?)—the boys began to call him Bart instead of Uncle Jim.
- Barrie's former wife Mary sold Black Lake Cottage and, after her second divorce, was out of money. Barrie arranged for her to have an income for life.
- During World War I, Barrie, along with other literary luminaries such as H. G. Wells, wrote articles to support the British war effort. He gave money to a hospital for soldiers and visited there to entertain them. He also established a home for children in France who had been wounded or orphaned in the war and paid for their needs.
- In 1929, Barrie gave the copyright and royalties from *Peter Pan* to the <u>Great Ormond Street Hospital for Sick Children</u> in perpetuity (forever). This has been a source of finances for them ever since.

- Barrie, because of severe cramping in his right hand, taught himself to write with his left hand. This is similar to Mark Twain's experience with arthritis in his right hand; he taught himself to write with his left hand.
- Sir James Matthew Barrie went to a convalescent home to recuperate from an illness but died in his sleep in the year <u>1937</u>. According to http://www.jmbarrie.co.uk, Nico, the youngest Davies boy (no longer a boy but in his 30s), was with him when he died.
- What happened to those five Davies boys who were the models for Peter Pan, the Darling brothers, and the lost boys? <u>George</u>, the oldest, was killed in World War I; John ("Jack") was sixty-five when he died just a few months before Peter died; Peter, a publisher and not happy to be identified as Peter Pan in his adulthood, threw himself under a train at age 63; Michael drowned in an accident at Oxford University, just shy of his twenty-first birthday; and the baby, Nicholas ("Nico"), died in in his 70s in 1980.

Sources for the material in Meet Sir Barrie: *J. M. Barrie and the Lost Boys: The Real Story Behind Peter Pan* by Andrew Birkin,[10]
J. M. Barrie: The Magic Behind Peter Pan by Susan Bivin Aller,[11]
http://www.jmbarrie.co.uk/,[12]
and, of course, http://en.wikipedia.org/wiki/J._M._Barrie.[13]

Lesson 3

Fun Facts

Teacher, your students are learning a few facts about the play and book *Peter Pan* and about the name Wendy, which did not exist until Barrie created it.

Literary Terms: Symbol and Motif

Teacher, this is a review of the term *symbol* and an introduction to the term *motif.*

In your Novel Notebook, make up the name for a new sports team and create a symbol or mascot for it. Then make a list of the qualities this new symbol stands for. For instance, the football team in Denver is called the Denver Broncos. Broncos are wild, untamed horses known for bucking, which makes them an appropriate name for a football team.

To download a FREE Novel Notebook with the questions already in it, go to http://writingwithsharonwatson.com/illuminating-literature-when-worlds-collide-gateway/ .

Teacher, students will also use the Novel Notebook to plot their life or an occurrence in their life as the hero's journey, which they will learn about in lesson 5.

Lesson 4

Writers' Devices: Tense and Prolepsis

Teacher, most stories are written in the past tense, and this is true of *Peter Pan*. However, for emphasis, Barrie switches to present tense in certain passages like the one in which he introduces the island denizens in "The Island Come True." Students are learning about this narrative shift. They are also learning about the anachronistic device called **prolepsis**, which is a flashforward.

Students also learn these terms: **narrative shift**, **tense**, and **anachronistic device**.

Read it This Way! No, Read it *This* Way!

Students are being reminded that there are two ways to read any story: (1) from the author's perspective and what the author intended the reader to understand, and (2) from the reader's own perspective, given the reader's experiences, beliefs, and so forth. Both are adequate readings. The first one will gain a deeper understanding of the story as it was meant to be, but it is legitimate to come to a story knowing nothing of its context and gaining meaning from it.

A warning: Beware of interpreting books only through the lens of gender, racial, or class/wealth/poverty issues and inequalities. While these issues often feature large in stories, interpreting stories through only those lenses is a narrow way to read a book. Look for the human element, not just the societal/what's-wrong-with-the-world perspective.

Yes, *Pudd'nhead Wilson* is about racial injustice, for example, but if you stop there, you will miss out on some deeply felt, real-life issues of living, like the lengths mothers will go to save their children.

Before Peter Pan There Was . . .

Students are learning about the Greek god Pan and the Roman god Faunus, both shepherd gods that were pranksters, and not in a nice way.

Suggested Reading and Homework Plan

Week 1:
- ❑ Complete lessons 1-4. Complete your Week 1 tasks if you have not already done so.

Week 2:
- ❑ Read the first eight chapters of *Peter Pan* ("Peter Breaks Through" – "The Mermaids' Lagoon").

Week 3:
- ❑ Read the last nine chapters of *Peter Pan* ("The Never Bird" – "When Wendy Grew Up").

90

Week 4:
- ❏ Rejoice! There is no activity this month!
- ❏ Complete lessons 5-8.

Stuff You Might Want to Know: Chapter by Chapter

Students are being guided through the book with tricky definitions, explanations of things that might be foreign to their experiences, and other things that will help them understand what they are reading.

They are also learning these writers' devices/literary terms: **deus ex machina**, **mirror scenes**, and **apostrophe**. They'll learn more about the term apostrophe in the next writers' devices section.

After You've Read the Book

Lesson 5

Five-Star Report

Students are filling out a graph to show how they felt about *Peter Pan*. 1 = Couldn't stand it. 5 = Loved it!

Reward: Distribute the small reward to each student who finished reading *Peter Pan*, perhaps Milky Way candy bars or Hershey's Kisses.

Colliding Worlds

What worlds are colliding with each other in *Peter Pan*? What people, philosophies, cultures, ideas, and so forth, are in conflict with each other? Fill in the list below. The first one is done for you.

(The following are possibilities. Your student may list others.)
1. *Pirates versus lost boys—Adults are dirty, disorganized, cruel, and unfair, and adulthood is harsh; youth is whimsical, fun, and softened by the ministrations of a mother.*
2. *Youth versus Age—Youth is preferable to age.*
3. *Immaturity and selfishness versus Maturity and selflessness—Maturity and selflessness are acceptable from time to time but not acceptable as a normal way of life—too stifling, requires too much responsibility and adult thinking.*
4. *Reality versus Imagination—Reality is stultifying and cloying; imagination is freedom.*
5. *Darlings versus Neverland—The pull of reality is stronger than the pull of imagination, even though reality is more depressing and harsher.*
6. *Time versus non-time (timelessness)—Time is our enemy only if we acknowledge its existence and demands.*

Okay, but what does it all *mean?* Sure, the pirates and the lost boys hate each other, but what does that signify in the story? Well, mateys, it shows the tension between age and youth, which is one of the themes of this story.

Next to the list you wrote above, write what you think Barrie is trying to tell you by putting that conflict into the story. *Answers are above and will vary.*

Conflicts

(The following are possibilities. Your student may list others.)
Peter Pan's Two Major Conflicts
1. *Peter versus Hook (another character). Hook is out to get Peter Pan because the boy had cut off his right hand and thrown it to the crocodile. Hook is also enraged by Peter's cockiness.*
2. *Peter versus himself or perhaps Peter versus nature. He doesn't want to grow up; he is in a race against time, which is his enemy. So he runs away.*

Wendy's Two Major Conflicts
1. *Wendy versus Tinker Bell (another character). Tinker Bell sees Wendy as competition from the moment she sees her, for they both like the same male—Peter Pan. Tinker Bell incites Tootles to shoot an arrow into Wendy. She has to be coerced into helping Wendy and the lost boys leave the island.*
2. *Wendy versus herself. She wants to be a part of the lost boys and of Peter Pan's life, but she also wants to grow up and become a wife and mother. Peter never catches on that she likes him. If he had, her feelings for him might have outweighed her desire for a normal adult life.*

Captain James Hook's Two Major Conflicts
1. *Hook versus the crocodile (nature). He obviously is terrified of the crocodile and avoids her at all costs.*
2. *Hook versus Peter Pan (another character). Hook hates Peter for his cockiness. He also hates him because he suspects that Peter has good form without really trying. Peter had been the person who had cut off his right hand and made him vulnerable to the crocodile. Peter also likes to play tricks on Hook; one is how Peter can sound like Hook and give orders. Eventually, Peter swears, "Hook or me this time."*

How could Barrie have made *Peter Pan* more exciting? *Answers will vary. Some possibilities: more adventures, giving Hook a different reason for hating Pan, giving them more of a history together, making Pan stay in London longer and try to live there, and so forth.*

What is wrong with the cover illustration? *The timing is off, which is amusing for a story about the advance of time. There was no crocodile at the ship during the fight. Wendy was not tied up at the time of the fight. Peter Pan was not scared, as he appears on the cover illustration. The illustration brings various elements together as though they were occurring at the same time.*

Writers' Devices: Apostrophe and Authorial Intrusion

Students are learning about the terms **apostrophe** and **authorial intrusion**.

Lesson 6

Complete the Online Quizzes and Survey

Objectives:
- To complete a fact quiz online for a grade to prove students read the book.
- To reinforce the terms they've learned so far in this text: tense, narrative shift, prolepsis, symbol, apostrophe, authorial intrusion, foreshadowing, conflict, context, *deus ex machina*, and mirror scenes.
- To complete questions online to express opinions, interpret events in *Peter Pan*, and ponder what they would do in similar circumstances.

The password to the quizzes and survey is BARRIE.

Teacher, students are instructed to go to http://WritingWithSharonWatson.com/illuminating-literature-when-worlds-collide-gateway/ to get links to complete the following:

- "Yes, I read it" quiz—graded online for you
- Literary Terms Quiz (tense, narrative shift, prolepsis, symbol, apostrophe, authorial intrusion, foreshadowing, conflict, context, *deus ex machina*, and mirror scenes)—graded online for you
- Opinion Survey—no grade, but answers to the opinion questions may help you develop a strategy for your discussion time.

Also, the quiz site will email a full report of the quiz (questions, your student's answers, the correct answers, and your student's grade) to the email address your student signed in with.

Teacher, if you prefer printed quizzes, you'll find them in *Illuminating Literature: When Worlds Collide, Quiz and Answer Manual,* available for sale at http://writingwithsharonwatson.com/illuminating-literature-when-worlds-collide.

Opinion questions have no correct answer; students are graded on participation. Their answers to the opinion questions may help you develop a strategy for your discussion time.

Teacher, students are allowed two attempts for the "Yes, I read it" quiz and the literary terms quiz but only one attempt for the opinion survey.

Vocabulary Quizzola for *Peter Pan*

Objectives:
- To reinforce good vocabulary habits and awareness.
- To gain a grade, which is separate from the Grading Grid.

Directions: Match the definition on the right with the correct word on the left. Write the letter of the definition in the blank next to the correct word.

The numbers after the words indicate page numbers where the words can be found in the Dover edition of *Peter Pan*. **Check with your teacher to see if this is an open-book quiz.** Correct answers are worth 5 points each.

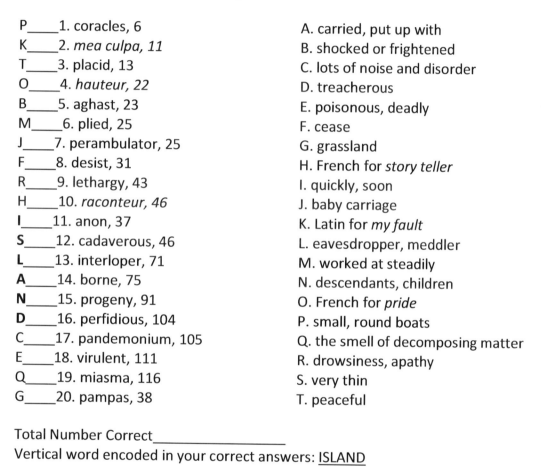

P____1. coracles, 6
K____2. *mea culpa, 11*
T____3. placid, 13
O____4. *hauteur, 22*
B____5. aghast, 23
M____6. plied, 25
J____7. perambulator, 25
F____8. desist, 31
R____9. lethargy, 43
H____10. *raconteur, 46*
I____11. anon, 37
S____12. cadaverous, 46
L____13. interloper, 71
A____14. borne, 75
N____15. progeny, 91
D____16. perfidious, 104
C____17. pandemonium, 105
E____18. virulent, 111
Q____19. miasma, 116
G____20. pampas, 38

A. carried, put up with
B. shocked or frightened
C. lots of noise and disorder
D. treacherous
E. poisonous, deadly
F. cease
G. grassland
H. French for *story teller*
I. quickly, soon
J. baby carriage
K. Latin for *my fault*
L. eavesdropper, meddler
M. worked at steadily
N. descendants, children
O. French for *pride*
P. small, round boats
Q. the smell of decomposing matter
R. drowsiness, apathy
S. very thin
T. peaceful

Total Number Correct_____
Vertical word encoded in your correct answers: <u>ISLAND</u>

Lesson 7

The Hero's Journey

Objective: To learn and identify the stages of the hero's journey plot in *Peter Pan*.

Teacher: Begin this lesson with the following questions and allow your students to think of answers.

Q: What is the purpose of the story to the main character? I mean, why does the writer have the hero go through all those troubles? *To grow or show a skill; to deal with fears, real or imagined inadequacies, or issues that have been haunting him; to become stronger, more compassionate, more courageous, and so forth; to serve as an example to others; to be tested to see what he's made of; to put him through sandpaper-on-raw-skin conflicts so he'll be transformed; to give him a chance to redeem himself, prove himself, learn from his mistakes, or accomplish something heroic, and so forth.*

Your students are learning these stages of the hero's journey, with explanations and examples of each stage spelled out in their textbook (key elements are in parentheses):

> › The Hero's Ordinary World [In literature class, this is called the *exposition*.]
> › The Call to Adventure (the call, the refusal, the inciting incident, mentor, traveling companions, gifts, warnings, powers)
> › Crossing the Threshold (threshold guardians)
> › Into the Journey's World (learn its rules, testing, acquire enemies and allies)
> › Into the Heart of the World [In literature class, this is called the *rising conflict* and *climax*.] (the inmost cave/belly of the beast, death-and-rebirth experience, supreme test or ordeal, reward or boon)
> › Crossing the Threshold to Return to the Ordinary World
> › The New Ordinary World [In literature class, this is called the *dénouement* or the *resolution*.] (character arc)

Teacher, students will pause after reading each stage of the hero's journey and answer a question about that stage of the plot as it occurs in *Peter Pan*.

Teacher, on the next page you'll find a graph that depicts what the hero's journey looks like. Draw it on the board for your students to see. Every story will deal with the stages of the hero's journey in a slightly different way. The image below is meant to be what the classic stages might look like.

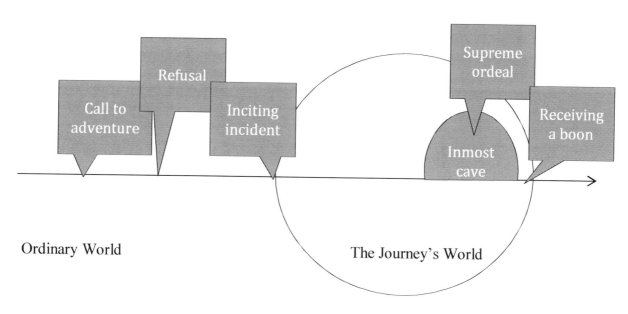

The hero's ordinary world

What is Peter Pan's stated goal on page 100? Write it here: *". . . I just want always to be a little boy and to have fun."*

The call to adventure

What is Peter Pan's **call to adventure**? (Hint: It comes from Wendy in chapter 3.) *"Don't go, Peter," she entreated, "I know such lots of stories."*

How does Peter **refuse the call** to adventure? *He grips her and draws her to the window. In one sense, he refuses his adventure entirely and, instead of entering his journey's world, he entices Wendy into his world, which to her is her journey's world. This may be the tragedy of Peter Pan, that he refuses the adventure while maintaining that he is having adventures. However, we'll consider Neverland to be the journey's world, for the sake of argument.*

What is Peter's **inciting incident**? *It's hard to say since he totally refuses the call to adventure. Again, for the sake of argument, if we consider Neverland to be the journey's world, let's say that it's when Peter realizes Mr. and Mrs. Darling are returning and the stars warn him of impending trouble by saying, "Cave, Peter!" This incites him to get the children out the nursery window.*

Who are Peter's **mentors**? Write your answer here: *He has none, which is another tragic thing about him, due to his refusal to grow up.*

What are Peter's **powers**? Write your answer here: *He can fly, understand Tinker Bell, cross freely from reality to Neverland. He's creative, cocky, imaginative, can think on his feet, and so forth.*

Crossing the threshold

When does Peter cross the threshold? Write your answer here: *When he flies out the nursery window with the Darling children in tow and eventually lands in Neverland. The crossing is not dangerous for Peter Pan but is quite dangerous for the children, who are hungry, occasionally fall, and are at times forgotten completely by Peter and left on their own.*

Who are Neverland's **threshold guardians**? Write your answer here: *the lost boys, who shoot down the Wendy bird.*

Into the journey's world

Who are Peter Pan's **enemies**? Write your answer here: *the pirates, the Indians, Hook, and TIME*

How does Peter **acquire allies**? Write your answer here: *He saves Tiger Lily and earns the grateful thanks of her tribe, who end up calling him the Great White Father.*

If the hero has an encounter with the antagonist early in this phase, it will go badly for the hero.

How does it go badly for Peter in his first meeting with Hook? *Even though Peter Pan saves Tiger Lily and Wendy, he is left on a rock to drown in the incoming tide. When he fights Hook there, he tries to be a fair fighter by offering his hand to Hook to pull him up, but Hook takes advantage of this and claws Peter's arm (symbolic of Peter cutting off Hook's hand?) with his hook, twice, instead. Not only is the boy physically hurt now but he is also rendered helpless. "Not the pain of this but its unfairness was what dazed Peter" (79).*

Who are Peter Pan's **shapeshifters**? Write your answer here: *Tinker Bell is sometimes a friend and sometimes not. Peter's mother, or his idea of a mother, is malleable, appearing kind in one memory and unkind in others.*

What is Peter Pan's **death-and-rebirth event**? Write your answer here: *Pan experiences a death-and-rebirth event when Tinker Bell drinks his poisoned medicine. This galvanizes him to fight Hook: "Hook or me this time" (115).*

Into the heart of the journey's world

What is Peter Pan's **supreme test**? Write your answer here: *His fight with Hook on Hook's turf, the pirate ship.*

What are Peter Pan's **rewards or boons**? Write your answer here: *He gains permission to come year after year to gather Wendy for his spring cleaning, when he remembers to do so. He continues to take Wendy's daughter and granddaughter back to Neverland for adventures (with whom? Hook is now dead) and spring cleaning. Wendy brings the lost boys back to the world of reality, but Barrie reports they were* *miserable as adults, which, strangely enough, seemed to be the fate of some of the real Davies boys as they grew up.*

Crossing the threshold to return to the ordinary world
This is often a dangerous time for the hero. In Peter Pan's case, it is a release of sorts until he crosses the threshold when Wendy is older. Then he suffers slightly.

The new ordinary world
What is the shape of Peter Pan's **character arc**? Write your answer here: *It's a flat, straight line. There's been absolutely no change whatsoever in his character, views, habits, and so forth.*

On the diagram, write these stages of the hero's journey as they appear in *Peter Pan*: the call to adventure, the refusal, the inciting incident, the inmost cave, and receiving the boon or reward.

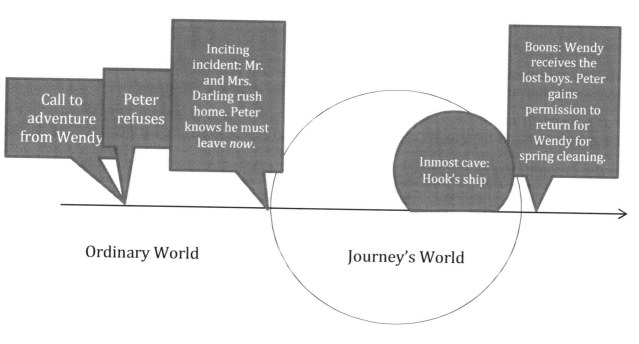

Lesson 8

Questions for Discussion

Teacher, before delving into the discussion questions, start with these:

  1. What questions do you have about *Peter Pan*?
  2. What aspects of this book appealed to you?
  3. What is your impression of this book?

These preliminary questions will help to clear up any misunderstandings or miscomprehensions from the books, and they'll get students talking during the discussion session because they are open-ended questions. Students can answer other students' questions, too. This pre-discussion time may also serve to answer some of the questions printed below or can be a springboard to any of the aspects of the book you want to focus on.

In addition, the answers to the opinion survey might give you an idea of what topics to focus on in your discussion time as well.

This discussion centers on growing up and becoming an adult and the consequences of not becoming a responsible adult.

1. The theme of growing up is introduced early in *Peter Pan*. On page 14, we find this: "Be a man, Michael!" Under what circumstances is this said? *Mr. Darling bucking up Michael to take his medicine just before Mr. Darling acts like a child in taking his own medicine. Thus, it is put in a negative light, being said by a hypocrite.*

2. **Josh** Birdwell, in "Shivaree Before Breakfast" from *The Friendly Persuasion*, defines growing up. Find what growing up means to him and write it here: *Growing up meant not being worried or scared any more. Meant having things just as they ought to be, the way you liked them, everything neat and happy—at last. If it didn't what was the use of being alive—taking the trouble to grow up?*

3. **Jess** Birdwell, in "Homer and the Lilies," tells how he knew he was an adult. Look it up and write it here: *"Why, Eliza, at eighteen I was a man. Owned a cow and horse and had cleared ten acres."*

4. Ernest Hemingway is purported to have written what a man must do to prove he's a man. On an index card or a small piece of paper, write what you think a boy must do to prove he's a man. Then on the other side of the card or paper, write out how a girl knows she's finally a woman. **After you've done that**, look on the next page to see what is in Hemingway's list. *Here's Hemingway's list: plant a tree, fight a bull, write a novel, father a son.* **Index cards** *may read "taking care of myself and others (being responsible for myself and others), having more patience than a kid (having delayed gratification), being aware of consequences and taking them into consideration when making decisions, being a role model," and so forth.* Do you agree with him? *Answers will vary.*

5. What are some coming-of-age rituals around the world or in history that move a boy to manhood in that culture? Why do you think there are more of these rituals for boys than there are for girls? *Answers will vary.*

6. When St. Paul said in I Corinthians 13 that he used to think and act as a child and then he put away childish things, what childish things do you think he put away? *Answers will vary.*

7. What happens to people when they remain lost boys (that is, don't put away childish things)? *Answers will vary, possibly having to do with what love isn't (instead of patient, impatient; instead of kind, unkind; and so forth).*

8. What's the difference between being childish and being childlike? *Answers will vary.*

9. Are teens afraid to grow up today? *According to my classes, the answers have been "Yes." Student loans, have to do everything themselves, life is suddenly dumped on you, have to make your own decisions, mortgages, and so forth.*
10. List some positive things you are looking forward to as an adult. *Answers will vary.*
11. How will you know when you are an adult? *Answers will vary.*
12. What qualities in adults you know would you like to emulate? *Answers will vary.*

Teacher, the grading grid for *Peter Pan* is on the next page. The grid is marked for a possible 100 points per book. Please feel free to adjust it to your needs and expectations. You have permission to copy it as many times as needed for your own class, co-op, reading group, book-of-the-month club, or family.

Grading Grid for *Peter Pan*

Student name: _____

Online "Yes, I read it" quiz, graded online. 1-10 points	
Online literary terms quiz, graded online. 1-10 points	
Participation in opinion questions online. 1-10 points	
Quality of participation in discussions. 1-25 points	
Successful completion of lessons and assignments. 1-25 points	
Finished reading the book. 1-20 points.	
Total grade for *Peter Pan*	

Writing with
Sharon Watson

Chapter 5: *Warriors Don't Cry*

Washington Square Press/Pocket Books   ISBN: 0-671-86639-7

Facebook Posts

If your group or co-op meets monthly, you may want to keep in touch with the students and keep them interested in the novels by creating a secret Facebook group for only them and their parents. Feel free to devise your own questions or find your own links to interesting material.

- If you were going to throw yourself into the middle of a huge ethical, political, or spiritual battle, what would it be?
- Read this fascinating interview with Melba Pattillo Beals and tell us what you think about her statement, "When you're a teenager, what you want most is to be welcomed." http://teacher.scholastic.com/barrier/hwyf/mpbstory/melchat.htm.
- These girls are twins! What would you like to ask these sisters? http://www.huffingtonpost.com/2015/03/02/biracial-twins-lucy-maria-aylmer_n_6787294.html?ncid=txtlnkusaolp00000592
- Explore this site or take a virtual tour of Central High School through the Little Rock Central High School National Historic Site, run by the National Park Service: http://www.nps.gov/chsc/learn/index.htm. Then come back and tell us one thing that intrigued you.
- Remember Minnijean and the chili incident in the cafeteria? Here's Oprah Winfrey with some of the Little Rock Nine as they face some of their tormentors: https://www.youtube.com/watch?v=8REh9ZlvBcw. Would you have been able to forgive that man?
- With all the social media available to us, do you think a torturous year like the one Melba and her friends endured is possible to a person or a group of people today?
- What question would you like to ask Melba Pattillo Beals?
- What question would you like to ask Melba's tormentors?

Before You Read the Book

Lesson 1

Suggested Reading and Homework Plan: Preview

Week 1:
 ❑ Complete lessons 1-2.
Week 2: Lesson 3

❏ Read Author's Note, Introduction: Little Rock Warriors Thirty Years Later, and chapters 1-9. Fill out any blanks and answer questions in your Novel Notebook pertaining to three of these chapters.

Week 3: Lesson 4
 ❏ Read chapters 10-19. Fill out any blanks and answer questions in your Novel Notebook pertaining to three of these chapters.

Week 4: Lesson 5
 ❏ Read chapters 20-28. Fill out any blanks and answer questions in your Novel Notebook pertaining to three of these chapters.

Week 5:
 ❏ Choose your activity and begin work on it. The list is at the end of this chapter.
 ❏ Complete lessons 6-10.
 ❏ Complete your activity. **Your teacher will tell you when this is due.**

Imitate!

Objectives:
 • To give students a chance to imitate a compare-and-contrast sentence.
 • To prompt students to look at their lives and write something real about it.

Read the first paragraph in chapter 1 of *Warriors Don't Cry*. Melba sets up the colliding worlds of stark opposites by beginning her memoir with a horrific compare-and-contrast statement. Be aware of those collisions and the opposites that she writes into her memoir.

Melba is mainly contrasting the types of activities her age mates were enjoying to the types of activities she and her fellow black students were enduring. She uses **parallelism** to achieve her stark contrast, leaning heavily on the past progressive tense ("was _____ing"):

While most other teenage girls were	listening, watching, and collecting,
Melba was	escaping, dodging, and washing.

Parallelism is a handy way of using the same sentence structure in two parts of a sentence or in two sentences. But its purpose is to contrast or to make the material easier to read and understand, as in the following example from the

Bible. Note that the sentence structure for both verses about being unfaithful to one's wife (Proverbs 6:27 and 6:28, NIV) is the same:

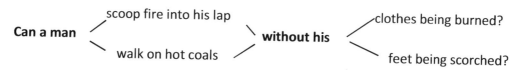

Write a paragraph of opposites in your life. Begin it with "While," as Melba does, if that helps you get going. Use parallel construction if that makes sense with what you are writing. Instead of simply scratching words onto a paper, try to say something meaningful about your life in your paragraph of contrasts.

Teacher: If you have time in class, you may want to use this as an in-class writing opportunity so students can learn by what their peers have written. If you are teaching a co-op, the paragraph can be due in a week or emailed to you.

Lesson 2

A Memoir

Students are learning a new genre: a **memoir** (pronounced mem • WAHR). It's in the nonfiction category.

Question in the text: List any memoirs you have read either for school or for pleasure. *Answers will vary.*

Meet Melba Pattillo Beals

Objectives:
- To give students a frame of reference (a context) from which to read *Warriors Don't Cry.*
- To show what Melba has done since the time of her memoir.

Teacher, students are reading about Beals' life.

In the spaces below, write two things about Melba's life that interested you: *Answers will vary.*

Fun Facts

Objectives:
- To connect the subject matter of *Warriors Don't Cry* to the topic of prejudice worldwide and throughout history.
- To understand that Christians are often seen in a negative light in media and entertainment, and not to let that influence students in a negative way against Christianity.

Students are learning that "documentary" films of the early 1940s portrayed Jews as vermin—filthy, swarming, disease-ridden. Filmmakers selected Jews who were ill or who had exaggerated facial features and presented them as what normal Jews looked like.

Question in the text: Are there any people groups today that are almost always shown on TV and in movies in a negative light? *Yes. In the United States, Christians and sometimes Jews are routinely portrayed in TV shows, movies, and novels as being stupid, weak-chinned, against science, "flat earthers," rigid, ignorant and loving it, angry, socially backward, and so forth. It is highly unusual in today's culture to find a priest, nun, minister, rabbi, or lay Christian portrayed as being normal, kind, generous, intelligent, and physically normal. Other than bosses and certain law-enforcement or government groups, it's hard to find a people group more maligned than Christians/Jews. Countries other than the United States will have other people groups routinely maligned.*

Students also are learning that the chestnut tree that stood outside Anne Frank's Secret Annex, where her family hid from the Nazis between 1942 and 1944 as recorded in her *Diary of a Young Girl*, has historical and symbolic significance today. Saplings from that very tree have been given to important historical sites around the world, and Central High School in Little Rock, Arkansas, is one of those sites.

In other exciting news: A commemorative coin was issued by the United States Mint in 2007 to honor the Little Rock Nine fifty years after their torturous first year of integration. One side of the one-dollar coin shows the feet of the students walking to school with a soldier. Nine stars line the image. Central High School adorns the other side of the coin.

Point of View and Voice

Objective: To become familiar with the term *voice*.

By definition, the point of view in any memoir is first person. Melba will be your first-person narrator throughout this year of terror. **Question in text:** What other books in this course have been in first person? *The War of the Worlds.*

Students are learning a new literary term: **voice**.

Publication and Other Info

In what year was *Warriors Don't Cry* published? <u>*1994*</u>

On page xvii, you will find why it took her so long to write this book. Please read that page and write why she waited so long: *"Now enough time has elapsed to allow healing to take place, enabling me to tell my story without bitterness."*

You will encounter the name NAACP frequently in *Warriors Don't Cry*. If you don't already know what this stands for, turn to page xx and write the full name of this organization in the blank: *National Association for the Advancement of Colored People.*

Appetizers

Objective: To set the stage for the story and to put it into a historical context.

Before you dig into the main course, please read pages xiii-xiv. You will eventually meet all these people in her narrative; however, the first two are the political movers and shakers who had much to do with the eventual integration in Little Rock, Arkansas. What do you think about a woman who would acknowledge students who "refused to torture us," even though they did nothing positive to help her? *Answers will vary.*

Now read the pages that follow the acknowledgments, all the way through page xxiii. Before proceeding with the book, write your preliminary impressions of the author: *Answers will vary.*

This is the end of lesson 2.

Suggested Reading and Homework Plan

Teacher: Let students know if this is the plan you want them to follow or if you have a different schedule in mind.

Week 1:
  ❑ Complete lessons 1-2. If you have not finished the tasks for Week 1 yet, finish them now.
Week 2: Lesson 3
  ❑ Read Author's Note, Introduction: Little Rock Warriors Thirty Years Later, and chapters 1-9. Fill out any blanks and answer questions in your Novel Notebook pertaining to three of these chapters.
Week 3: Lesson 4
  ❑ Read chapters 10-19. Fill out any blanks and answer questions in your Novel Notebook pertaining to three of these chapters.
Week 4: Lesson 5
  ❑ Read chapters 20-28. Fill out any blanks and answer questions in your Novel Notebook pertaining to three of these chapters.
Week 5:
  ❑ Choose your activity and begin work on it. The list is at the end of this chapter.
  ❑ Complete lessons 6-10.
  ❑ Complete your activity. **Your teacher will tell you when this is due.**

As you did with *The Friendly Persuasion*, you will pause at the end some of these chapters to respond to them. The chapters are short and go quickly. Keep your **Novel Notebook** with you, for you will be using it as you answer questions.
There are too many questions to answer all of them. Choose **three chapters from each section** (I've divided the book up into three sections for the three weeks you'll be reading it) and answer the questions from those chapters.

You will note that the chapters are not titled; they are simply numbered. Name your nine chapters according to their content and what sticks out to you about them.

Lesson 3

Author's Note – Chapter 9

Teacher, this is a week-long lesson. Students are advised to pace themselves.

Students are choosing three of the chapters in this first section to respond to. The questions are repeated in their Novel Notebooks.

To download a FREE Novel Notebook with the questions already in it, go to http://writingwithsharonwatson.com/illuminating-literature-when-worlds-collide-gateway/ .

Chapter 1
Your new title: _____ *Answers will vary*.
1. Melba's grandmother India believed that since Melba easily could have died in infancy, God had spared her life for a reason. Do you have a story similar to Melba's, a life-and-death experience? Write it in your Novel Notebook. Do you agree with Grandma India that there's a reason God spared your life? Explain.
2. Melba writes: "I became an instant adult, forced to take stock of what I believed and what I was willing to sacrifice to back up my beliefs. The experience endowed me with an indestructible faith in God" (page 2). Have you ever had to take stock of what you believe and what you are willing to sacrifice in order to back up your beliefs? If so, how has it changed or strengthened your faith in God? Write your answers in your Novel Notebook.

Chapter 2
Your new title: _____ *Answers will vary*.
Choose two of the following to write more about in your Novel Notebook:

1. Melba wrote letters to God when she was young about her hopes and the inequities she saw all around her. This was nothing new. King David often wrote psalms to God about his hopes and the nasty things he was seeing or experiencing. Now it's your turn to write to God. In your Novel Notebook, write your own letter or psalm.

2. Melba remembered some seminal events in her life, even as a young child of four or five years of age. Recall an important event from your childhood and write it in your Novel Notebook.

3. Grandma India tells Melba, "You don't want to be white, what you really want is to be free, and freedom is a state of mind." Do you agree with Grandma India? Explain.

4. What are your gut reactions to Melba's stories about her trip to the merry-go-round, her experiences with the "White Ladies" restroom, and her father who could not help her mother for fear of retaliation?

Chapter 3
Your new title: _____ *Answers will vary.*

What was Melba's motivation to sign up to go to Central High School? *Curiosity—she wanted to see the inside of the school and other buildings blacks were not allowed to enter (p. 28). Opportunity—Central High had newer books, nice equipment, and different classes, and Melba wanted better educational opportunities for her future.*

Chapter 4
Your new title: _____ *Answers will vary.*

1. What year in school was Melba when she entered Central High School? *A junior (p. 34)*
2. How did whites react to the integration news? *Hostile, negative, threats, organized and fought it, fired blacks and retaliated in other ways (pp. 34, 36, 39, 63, and others)*
3. How did blacks react to the integration news? *Fear, anger, disapproval, pride, called her "uppity," asked why she would want to go where she wasn't wanted (pp. 31, 32, 36, 38, 47, 63, 84, and others)*

Chapter 5
Your new title: _____

Chapter 6
Your new title: _____
Do you agree with Grandma India's statement that "God's warriors don't cry, 'cause they trust that he's always by their side"? Explain in your Novel Notebook.

Chapter 7
Your new title: _____
Humor has great power to ease tensions, as Ernest Green and Terrence Roberts demonstrated. Recall a time when humor came to your rescue in this way or when you used it on someone's behalf. What did it defuse? Write the incident in your Novel Notebook.

Chapter 8

Your new title: _____ *Answers will vary.*

1. "Freedom is not integration. Freedom is being able to go with Grandma to the wrestling matches," writes Melba in her notebook. What is freedom to you? Finish the following sentence in your Novel Notebook: "Freedom is...." Explain.

2. Melba hears people praying for her and knows that when she needs help, the church will be her network. Recall a time when you knew someone was praying for you. How did that affect you? Write it in your Novel Notebook. Or recall a time when you prayed for someone. Write what happened.

On page 83 you will find a very poignant simile, and on page 88 you will find a clever one. Write them in your Novel Notebook. *"It pained my insides to see, once again, the twisted, scowling white faces with open mouths jeering, clustered about my friend's head like bouquets of grotesque flowers." (p. 83) "Thoughts buzzed inside my head like bees disturbed in their hive." (p. 88)*

Chapter 9

Your new title: _____ *Answers will vary.*

On page 96 you will notice how evolution helped to demean black people by comparing them to something. What is the name? *Monkeys.*

Lesson 4

Chapters 10-19

Teacher, this is a week-long lesson. Students are advised to pace themselves.

Students are choosing three of the following chapters to respond to in their Novel Notebooks.

Chapter 10

Your new title: _____ *Answers will vary.*

1. In your Novel Notebook, write your reactions to Melba's first morning in Central High School.

2. On page 108 you will find a simile that accentuates the world of opposites that Melba began in the first paragraph. Find it and write it in your Novel Notebook. *"The rumble of the crowd was like that at a football game when the hero runs the ball to the end zone for a touchdown—only this time, none of the voices were cheering."*

Chapter 11

Your new title: _____ *Answers will vary.*

On pages 122-3 you will find an article Melba wrote. It is an extremely positive spin on a very negative and dangerous event. Think back to a horrible day in your life and write an article in your Novel Notebook about it in as positive a light as you can, following Melba's example, without lying. This is not to minimize the event or the pain; it is to try to understand Melba and her predicament.

Chapter 12
Your new title: _____ *Answers will vary.*

Chapter 13
Your new title: _____ *Answers will vary.*

1. On pages 136 and 141, you will find two analogies ("It was like . . .") that highlight the world of opposites that Melba was living in. Find these two similes and write them here. *"It was like being on a peaceful island." (p. 136) "Entering the door was like walking into a zoo with the animals outside their cages." (p. 141)*

2. "Would you like to be white?" Aside from the insensitivity of this question, consider the deeper meaning of the reporter's question to Melba. Most people are the underdog in some undertaking—a sports team, their size, their intelligence, their birth order, their belief that the Bible is the true Word of God—just to name a few. Change the reporter's question: "Would you like to be _____?" How will you finish the question? Would you like to be smarter, richer, quicker, taller? Answer your own question. Do you like Melba's answer? Record your answers in your Novel Notebook.

Chapter 14
Your new title: _____
"Disciplined, crisp, precise, confident, and powerful." Those five words describe the 101st Airborne Division sent to help the Little Rock Nine. Choose five words to describe Melba's integration experience so far. Then choose five words to describe the whites' attitudes toward integration. *Answers will vary. Possibly harrowing, torturous, unfair, unjust, and so on.*

Chapter 15
Your new title: _____ *Answers will vary.*
Do you agree with Danny's advice on page 161? Explain in your Novel Notebook.

Chapter 16
Your new title: _____ *Answers will vary.*
1. What simile describes the Arkansas National Guard on page 168? Find the simile. *"Just then, I noticed the members of the Arkansas National Guard lounging against the walls like cats in sunlight."*

2. Remember Melba's five-word description of the 101st Airborne Division in Chapter 14 (page 146)? Here is another opposite for you: Find the description of the

Arkansas National Guard and the comments Melba's friends make about them in this chapter. Write the adjectives, nouns, and verbs they use to describe these men: *Biggest, dumbest, most disheveled hayseeds, looked as if they had slept in their rumpled uniforms, clods, shuffled out, a ridiculous wagging tail.*

3. Melba often heard voices of wise council in her head when she was in trouble (Grandma India, Danny, and so on). Who are your voices of wise council when you need a quick word in your ear? Write them in your Novel Notebook.

Chapter 17
Your new title: _____ *Answers will vary.*

Chapter 18
Your new title: _____ *Answers will vary.*

Chapter 19
Your new title: _____ *Answers will vary.*
   1. Melba writes about wanting to shoot a machine gun off over her attackers' heads, even though she knows that guns aren't allowed, even in her thoughts. These students had to deal with tremendous amounts of anger and pain as a natural reaction to being abused by students and betrayed by adults. What do you do when you're angry? What are some healthy ways of dealing with anger? Write these in your Novel Notebook.
   2. Read the advice Melba's mother gave her on page 210. Do you agree with her? Explain in your Novel Notebook.

Lesson 5

Chapters 20-28

Teacher, this is a week-long lesson. Students are advised to pace themselves.

Students are choosing three of these chapters to respond to.

Chapter 20
Your new title: _____ *Answers will vary.*
Write your reaction in your Novel Notebook to Melba not helping Minnijean on page 219.

Chapter 21
Your new title: _____ *Answers will vary.*
Integration (mainly, the white segregationists' reactions to it) took many things away from Melba's life. On page 2 she mentions that it took her childhood. It took her sweet sixteen birthday party, too. What are the other things stolen from Melba during this difficult year? Write them in your Novel Notebook and be on the lookout

for a few more she mentions in later chapters. *Innocence, girlhood, "warm sweet self" that made her a person, her Christmas shopping fun, her trust in people, her normalcy, her time with her boyfriend, her old friends, her extra-curricular activities, herself— "Melba went away to hide"(p. 246), a year of being a teenager (p. 305)*

Chapter 22

Your new title: _____ *Answers will vary.*
"I wish I were dead," writes Melba in her notebook. When she finally tells Grandma India, what is that woman's response? What would you say or write to a friend who is contemplating suicide or who is very down? Write it in your Novel Notebook.

Chapter 23

Your new title: _____ *Answers will vary.*
"Dignity is a state of mind, just like freedom." Do you agree with Grandma India's statement? Explain. Do you agree with Grandma India's brand of fighting back (page 242)? Explain in your Novel Notebook.

Chapter 24

Your new title: _____ *Answers will vary.*

Chapter 25

Your new title: _____ *Answers will vary.*

Chapter 26

Your new title: _____ *Answers will vary.*
What do you think about Link and his on-again, off-again actions? Write your response in your Novel Notebook.

Chapter 27

Your new title: _____ *Answers will vary.*

Chapter 28

Your new title: _____ *Answers will vary.*
1. Melba records a fire ceremony on pages 302-3. Many health professionals would agree with Grandma India in the healing powers of naming those who have wronged you and then forgiving them as the fire burns up their names. If you were to have a forgiving fire ceremony, whose names would you write down and burn up? Write the names and, if possible, have your own forgiving fire ceremony.
2. Write the metaphor by which Melba describes the McCabe family (page 307). *"But they became the loving, nurturing bridge over which I walked to adulthood."*
3. Melba uses another metaphor when talking about Link (page 311). Write it in your Novel Notebook along with people in your life who have been "special

gifts from God." *Link was one of those "special gifts from God sent to ferry me over a rough spot in my life's path."*

4. Formerly, you listed the things Melba lost during her horrible year of integration. Now list the things she gained from her torturous experiences at Central High School in Little Rock, Arkansas, according to her. *The guidance and unconditional love of the McCabes, "a positive force that changed the course of my life," courage, patience, "we are not separate." (pp.307, 312)*

After You've Read the Book

Lesson 6

Five-Star Report

Students are filling out a graph to show how they felt about *Warriors Don't Cry*. 1 = Couldn't stand it. 5 = Loved it!

Reward: Distribute the small reward to each student who finished reading *Warriors Don't Cry*, perhaps white/dark chocolate (something that signifies racial tension) or Cadbury eggs to tie in to the egg-in-the-hair incident.

Colliding Worlds

Here are some possibilities:

1. *Violence and rage versus peace-making and forgiveness*
2. *White versus Black*
3. *The federal government versus the state government*
4. *Segregation versus integration*
5. *A healthy, normal life versus an abusive, tortured, fearful year*

What negative things happen when these worlds collide? Write your answer below: *violence, the need for self-defense, torture, loss of friends, loss of a normal childhood or a normal year in school, loss of innocence, and so on.*

What positive things happen when these worlds collide? Write your answer below: *White schools become integrated, Melba grows stronger and learns how to deal with personal violence, they make the way for other white institutions to become integrated, and so on.*

Which of these conflicts could have been prevented? Choose one and explain below: *Answers will vary.*

Which of these conflicts have you experienced in your life? Explain below: *Answers will vary.*

Order Up

Put the following important events from *Warriors don't Cry* into the correct chronological order by putting numbers in the blanks below:

_3_1. Governor Faubus calls the National Guard to Central High.

_5_2. President Eisenhower orders Governor Faubus to cooperate with the Supreme Court and integrate.

_1_3. The Supreme Court rules in the case of *Brown v. Board of Education of Topeka, Kansas*, which starts the integration ball rolling.

_8_4. Governor Faubus closes all Little Rock high schools to deter integration.

_7_5. The 101st Airborne Division arrives in Little Rock to make sure the integration moves along without violence.

_2_6. Little Rock's Central High school board makes plans to integrate on a limited basis.

_4_7. Melba, Elizabeth, and the rest of the Little Rock Nine try to go to school but are kept out by the National Guard and white mobs.

_6_8. The Little Rock Nine actually get inside Central High School, but only for a morning.

Vocabulary Quizzola for *Warriors Don't Cry*

Objectives:
- To reinforce good vocabulary habits and awareness.
- To gain a grade, which is separate from the Grading Grid.

Directions: Match the definition on the right with the correct word on the left by entering the letter in the correct blank. Numbers after the words indicate the page number on which that word can be found in the official version for this course of *Warriors Don't Cry*. **Ask your teacher if this is an open-book quiz.** Each correct answer is worth 5 points.

_F_1. Kowtow, 15	A. to suffocate
_R_2. Incendiary, 90	B. the likeness of a person, a form to be burned
_K_3. Aspirations, 122	C. harsh and biting
_G_4. Quash, 124	D. a go-between
_O_5. Placid, 134	E. unkempt, untidy
_C_6. Scathing, 135	F. to abase oneself in a demeaning way
_Q_7. Demise, 144	G. to stop or quell
_N_8. Complement, 147	H. excluded, left out of someone's society
M_9. Fiasco, 165	I. a stipulation or condition
E_10. Disheveled, 171	J. a bitter scolding
L_11. Belligerent, 172	K. hopes and dreams
B_12. Effigy, 174	L. warlike, angry, hostile
A_13. Asphyxiate, 178	M. a complete and utter failure
_H_14. Ostracized, 190	N. a full amount

_S_ 15. Furor, 193
_P_ 16. Adamant, 194
_J_ 17. Lambasting, 222
_T_ 18. Fracas, 225
_I_ 19. Proviso, 233
_D_ 20. Liaison, 235

O. calm
P. unyielding
Q. death or failure
R. inflammatory, inciting to high emotion
S. excitement, commotion, hubbub
T. disturbance, argument

The vertical encoded word in the correct answers: MELBA

Lesson 7

Melba and the Hero's Journey

Teacher, you may want to do this together in class. Students might get more out of it and understand it better if you do it together as a group. What one student won't know, another will.

In the spaces below, tell where the stages and elements from the hero's journey occur in for Melba.

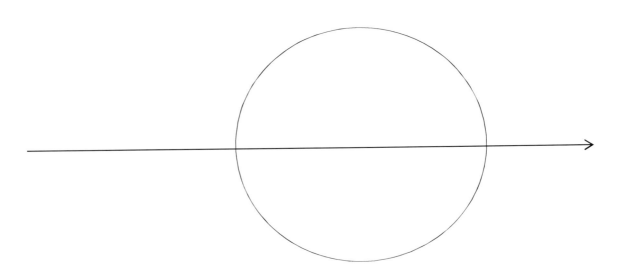

The hero's journey diagram

Explanations of the stages and elements of the hero's journey as Melba experienced them:
Exposition—*chapters 1-3, tensions between black and white communities, mistreatment of and violence against blacks, family situations and members*
Call to Adventure—*when Melba signs the paper in school agreeing to integrate (p. 28)*

Refusing the Call—*when Melba pleads with her mother to let her live with relatives in Cincinnati after tasting a bit of freedom and calm relations between black and white folks (p. 31)*

Inciting Incident—*more of a realization that she doesn't want to let down the other students who signed up as well (p. 45)*

Crossing the Threshold into the World of Adventure—*is rebuffed that first day by mobs of angry white people and by the Arkansas National Guard and can't stay in Central High more than an hour the second time (chapters 5 and 10)*

Gifts—*born on an important day (the original Pearl Harbor Day) and almost died ("You're supposed to carry this banner for our people" p. 5), her feisty spirit, her determination, her positive outlook on life, her ability to learn and be flexible, her mother and grandmother, her ability to communicate through her writing*

Mentors—*her mother, grandmother, NAACP attorney Thurgood Marshall (who later became a Supreme Court justice), Arkansas NAACP state president Daisy Bates*

Traveling Companions—*the other Little Rock Nine, occasionally*

Enemies—*the man who almost raped Melba upon hearing of the Supreme Court's decision in* Brown v. the Board of Topeka, Kansas *decision; the grocery store owner Mr. Waylan; phone callers; rock throwers; shooters; the students in Central High who beat, attacked, stabbed, threw acid on, tripped, walked on heels; the angry white mobs; the mothers who broke into the school; the Arkansas National Guard; Governor Faubus; most of the white community in Little Rock*

Allies—*shorthand teacher Mrs. Pickwick, some of the Central High students, the couple who rescued Elizabeth and who set up tutoring sessions for the nine while they waited to go to school, the policemen in those early days of trying to get into the school, the 101st Airborne Division, reporters*

Enemies turned into Allies—*Link, some of the white community*

Shapeshifters—*Link, Marsha (her friend from the "old days"), the girl who wanted her picture taken with Melba during the Pledge of Allegiance*

First Encounter with the Enemy Going Badly—*angry white mobs threaten to hang Melba and her mother as Melba and the other Nine try to enter Central High*

Death-and-Rebirth Event—*her Sweet Sixteen birthday party, when her old friends would not attend and no one comes but Vince. In fact, her old friends are having a Christmas party without inviting her. "[Y]ou'all are just not one of us anymore. You stuck your necks out, but we're not willing to die with you" (p. 216). She realizes her old life is gone. In fact, she wonders what she has left and who she is. She wants to be "just plain Melba" (p. 214), but "the integration had stolen my sixteenth birthday (p. 217).*

Supreme Ordeal—*In Melba's case, there is not one event but a ramping up of attacks and a loss of her selfhood. After Minnijean is expelled and moves to New York, "the segregationists went wild" (p. 245). Melba writes in her journal, "I think only the warrior exists in me now. Melba went away to hide. She was too frightened to stay here" (p. 246). The number and viciousness of the attacks increased from Easter to graduation. She is burned with firecrackers, receives death threats, and has a price on her head. Can she make it to the end of the school year?*

Crossing the Threshold to Return to Ordinary World—*Melba moves away from Little Rock to Santa Rosa, California, to live with Dr. George McCabe and his family (p. 307).*

Boon or Reward—*Her ability to deal with attacks, her new reliance on God and others for strength, her skills and experience in journalism, "courage and patience" (p. 312).*

Resolution—*Grandma India's death, Melba's move to California to live with a Quaker family; a few pages of her college experience and her marriage; her daughter (pp. 306-312).*

Lesson 8

Literary Terms: Analogy, Euphemism, and Hyperbole

Objective: To learn the terms analogy, euphemism, and hyperbole.

Students are learning a few new literary terms, all of which are in the category of figurative language: **analogy**, **euphemism**, and **hyperbole**.

Literary Elements

Literary elements are simply the ingredients that make up a story, poem, or play: plot, character, theme, setting, tone, mood, point of view, style, voice, and—yes—conflict.

Lesson 9

Complete the Online Quizzes and Survey

Teacher, students are instructed to go to http://WritingWithSharonWatson.com/illuminating-literature-when-worlds-collide-gateway/ to get links to complete the following:

- "Yes, I read it" quiz—graded online for you
- Literary Terms Quiz (memoir, analogy, euphemism, hyperbole, hero's journey, voice, and literary elements)—graded online for you
- Opinion Survey—no grade, but answers to the opinion questions may help you develop a strategy for your discussion time.

Students are allowed two attempts with each quiz and one with the opinion survey. Also, the quiz site will email a full report of the quiz (questions, your student's answers, the correct answers, and your student's grade) to the email address your student signed in with.

Password for *Warriors Don't Cry* quizzes and opinion survey: BEALS.

Teacher, if you prefer printed quizzes, you'll find them in *Illuminating Literature: When Worlds Collide, Quiz and Answer Manual,* available for sale at http://writingwithsharonwatson.com/illuminating-literature-when-worlds-collide.

Opinion questions have no correct answer; students are graded on participation. Their answers to the opinion questions may help you develop a strategy for your discussion time.

Teacher, students are allowed two attempts for the "Yes, I read it" quiz and the literary terms quiz but only one attempt for the opinion survey.

Lesson 10

Questions for Discussion

Teacher, before delving into the discussion questions, open the floodgates with these questions:

> 1. What questions do you have about *Warriors Don't Cry*?
> 2. What aspects of this book appealed to you?
> 3. What is your impression of this memoir?

These preliminary questions will help to clear up any misunderstandings or miscomprehensions from the books, and they'll get students talking during the discussion session because they are open-ended questions. Students can answer other students' questions, too. This pre-discussion time may also serve to answer some of the questions printed below or can be a springboard to any of the aspects of the book you want to focus on.

In addition, the answers to your students' opinion survey might give you a direction you want to take your discussion time.

Also, feel free to pull any questions from the chapter questions to discuss. Chances are that students did not deal with all of them as they were only supposed to choose nine chapters in total to answer.

Questions on the topic of dealing with violence:

1. What methods did Melba, her mother, Grandma India, and others in her community use to deal with violence? *Praying, singing hymns, memorizing Scripture and reciting it aloud or silently when needed, asking for advice from her mother and grandmother, staying connected to her Little Rock Nine group, attending NAACP and Little Rock Nine meetings, calling friends, thanking an aggressor when egg was thrown on her, defending herself with a wrestling move when she was attacked, running or walking swiftly away, staying alert, trying to get help when she could, making light of situations when possible, putting situations in a positive light when*

possible, writing in her diary, trying to maintain as normal a life as possible, having something to look forward to, listening to elders when they said it was too dangerous to leave the house, trying to influence the black community through discussions and the white community by trying not to make waves, putting on a stoic front in public, crying in private, being an example by integrating the university, employing Gandhi's passive resistance methods, defending the family with a shotgun, being vigilant, employing police and other troops when possible, keeping her head up and her posture straight to show her dignity, trying to make friends of some of the aggressors, concealing emotions, smiling, forgiving, leaving the area so she can heal in a calm setting.

2. Which ones were the most successful? *It seems that the variety of methods Melba, her mother, and her grandmother employed made it possible for Melba to finish the year at Central High. Each method was successful in its turn, and she needed a variety to give her success.*

3. How have you dealt with violence? Was your method successful? Answers *will vary.*

4. "The robb'd that smiles, steals something from the thief." What does this quote from William Shakespeare mean, and how does it relate to *Warriors Don't Cry*? *If we don't react in the way the thief expects, we have stolen some satisfaction from him. This quote reminds readers of the time Melba said thank you to the person who threw an egg at her.*

5. Thurgood Marshall, whom you met in *Warriors Don't Cry* as an attorney for the NAACP and who later became the first African American to sit on the Supreme Court of the United States, once said, "Lawlessness is lawlessness. Anarchy is anarchy. Neither is an excuse." What do you think he meant? *Answers will vary.*

6. Melba's dad felt powerless to protect his wife and family when they were threatened; he knew there would be retaliation to himself, his family, and the whole black community. What does it do to a man when he cannot defend and protect his family? What does it do to a community when the men cannot protect their women and children without fear of retaliation? *Answers will vary, but generally it tears down their sense of manhood, it attacks their core and emasculates them; it pushes them to give up since there is no good way to protect and still have a good outcome. They feel like failures, powerless, and often abandon their families.*

Question on the topic of judging people by their physical appearance:

1. What steps can you take to avoid being negative toward people who are physically different from you? (physical handicap, different color skin, beautiful, not so beautiful, have a physical anomaly or attribute others like to laugh at, fashion impaired, speech impediment, learning disability, no learning disabilities, and so forth) *Answers will vary.* **Teacher,** *if you have an example of one time when you*

learned not to judge people by some outward or mental-ability value, share it with the class. Invite the class to share their stories as well.

Questions on the topic of having a personal network:

1. Do you have a variety of people you can rely on in times of great stress or distress? How do you develop a personal network? *Answers will vary.*

2. How true is the title of this memoir? *Warriors don't cry in public and they try not to be whiny babies and complain all the time. However, Melba felt emotional release when she was able to cry in private upon occasion. Students likely will have a variety of opinions on this topic.*

Compare and contrast:
Warriors Don't Cry and *Pudd'nhead Wilson:* In your opinion, which one of these books has the stronger message against racism? Explain. Which one made a stronger impact on you? Explain. *Answers will vary.*

If You Liked This Book

Students are reading a list of books similar to *Warriors Don't Cry* in theme and topic.

This is the end of lesson 10.

Your Choice of Activities

Teacher, let your students know when this is due.

Note: Choose ONE of the following activities. **Read all of them** carefully before you make your decision. Below you will find a short explanation of each activity:

- Be the Author—Write a short story.
- Sell the Book—Write the blurb and a review to sell the book to the public.
- Say it in Song—Write a song.
- You Are the Expert—Read about Gandhi and write a short report.
- History Buff—Find out about other integration stories of the time period.
- History Buff II—Write a radio news release.
- Explore—Read other black writers.
- The Artist in You—Draw, paint, sculpt, or create a mural.

Below are the activities. Choose one. Dig in.

Be the Author
Write a short story in which certain people are discriminated against for something arbitrary—people who wear glasses versus people who don't, people

who are red headed versus people who aren't, left-handers versus right-handers, and so forth. How does the minority group cope? Gain respect? Gain equality (if ever)?

Sell the Book

You work in the marketing or promotion department of a major publisher, and it is your job to sell *Warriors Don't Cry* to the public. Write the blurb (the part on the back of the book that coaxes potential readers) and write a book review that will be published on the publisher's Website.

Say it in Song

Write a song about something you encountered in *Warriors Don't Cry* and sing it for an interested audience.

You Are the Expert

On page 210 in *Warriors Don't Cry*, Melba learns about Gandhi. Research the man and his beliefs. Learn why Grandma India thought he was so important. Write a short report on what you find.

History Buff

Little Rock, Arkansas, is not the only town in the United States that had integration problems. Research other towns and what happened there during this important time period. Were their experiences similar, better, or worse than Little Rock's? Write a short report or give a short speech to an interested listener about what you find.

History Buff II

Schools were not the only place where blacks were not initially welcome. Black actors for the theater and movies were consistently segregated from white actors and given small, stereotypic roles. The armed services and even sports teams kept people segregated for a long time.

Learn about a pioneer of integration in any of these areas or in others. Then write a radio announcement about the person and the event as though the announcement were a news release of the day.

Explore

Read a book by another black author or poet. Then write about what shocked, interested, or moved you. The following list will help you get you started:

Charles W. Chesnutt   Paul Lawrence Dunbar
Langston Hughes   Ann Spencer
James Weldon Johnson   Countee Clemen
Maya Angelou   Miss Lucille Clifton
Georgia Douglas Johnson   Miss Mari Evans

The Artist in You

Paint, draw, sculpt, or create a mural to highlight something you read in this book. Show it to an interested adult or display it in a school or community event.

Teacher, the grading grid for *Warriors Don't Cry* is on the next page. The grid is marked for a possible 100 points per book. Please feel free to adjust it to your needs and expectations. You have permission to copy it as many times as needed for your own class, co-op, reading group, book-of-the-month club, or family.

The Grading Grid for *Warriors Don't Cry*

Student Name: _____

Online "Yes, I read it" quiz, graded online. **1-10 points**	
Online literary terms quiz, graded online. **1-10 points**	
Participation in opinion questions online. **1-10 points**	
Quality of participation in discussions. **1-20 points**	
Successful completion of lessons and assignments. **1-20 points**	
Successful completion of activity. **1-10 points**	
Finished reading the book. **1-20 points.**	
Total grade for *Warriors Don't Cry*	

Writing with Sharon Watson

Chapter 6: *A Tale of Two Cities*

Dover Thrift Edition   ISBN 0-486-40651-2

Facebook Posts

If your group or co-op meets monthly, you may want to keep in touch with the students and keep them interested in the novels by creating a secret Facebook group for only them and their parents. Feel free to devise your own questions or find your own links to interesting material.

- Go to this site and tell us something you learned about Charles Dickens there that you did not know before: http://www.biography.com/people/charles-dickens-9274087
- What other books by Charles Dickens have you read? What did you think about them?
- The guillotine—or the National Barber—features large in this novel. What do you think of this form of capital punishment?
- If you could be a character in this book, which one would you be and why?
- Here's a YouTube video about a creepy topic: the guillotine. Watch it and tell us your reactions: https://www.youtube.com/watch?v=Qi6TTn35BrY
- In this "best of times/worst of times" novel, love wins over hatred and vengeance. Tell about a time in your life when love proved stronger than something negative. (*Love* can be love of family, brothers and sisters, parents, country, church, political or ethical ideal, friends, something in nature, and so forth.)
- Lucie Manette had an intuition that something bad was going to happen. Have you ever had an intuition about something good or bad? What happened?
- Here is a scene from a movie version of *A Tale of Two Cities*: https://www.youtube.com/watch?v=DTqv1fPQ5Y8. What are your reactions to this scene?
- It is interesting to note that Dickens does not have Lucie Darnay and Madame Defarge face off as equals in the end. This encounter would not fly with today's editors. The main protagonist *has* to battle the main antagonist. She cannot confront her nemesis through her old nurse. Good has to meet evil—and gain some sort of victory. How would you have these two women face off?
- If you could talk with one of the characters in the book, which one would it be and what would you talk about?
- What question would you like to ask Charles Dickens?

Before You Read the Book

Lesson 1

Write the first twelve words from the book: *It was the best of times, it was the worst of times.*

Write the last paragraph from the book: *"It is a far, far better thing that I do, than I have ever done; it is a far, far better rest that I go to than I have ever known."*

Suggested Reading and Homework Plan: Preview

Week One:
- ❏ Complete lessons 1-3.
- ❏ Complete lesson 4: Read Book the First (chapters 1-6). Answer questions from this section in your Novel Notebook.

Week Two: Lesson 5
- ❏ Read Book the Second (chapters 1-24) in the middle of the book. Answer questions from this section in your Novel Notebook.

Week Three: Lesson 6
- ❏ Read Book the Third (chapters 1-15) at the end of the book. Answer questions from this section in your Novel Notebook.

Week Four:
- ❏ Choose your activity (see the end of the chapter) and begin work on it.
- ❏ Complete lessons 7-8.
- ❏ Complete your activity. Your teacher will tell you when this is due.

Imitate!

The settings are so important in this novel that you are going to try your hand at creating a setting. Read the following paragraphs from Book the Second, chapter 9, "The Gorgon's Head," and notice the words Dickens uses to create the effect or mood of impending death:

> It was a heavy mass of building, that chateau of Monsieur the Marquis, with a large stone court-yard before it, and two stone sweeps of staircase meeting in a stone terrace before the principal door. A stony business altogether, with heavy stone balustrades, and stone urns, and stone flowers, and stone faces of men, and stone heads of lions, in all directions. As if the Gorgon's head had surveyed it, when it was finished, two centuries ago.

. . . The great door clanged behind him, and Monsieur the Marquis crossed a hall grim with certain old boar-spears, swords, and knives of the chase; grimmer with certain heavy riding-rods and riding-whips, of which many a peasant, gone to his benefactor Death, had felt the weight when his lord was angry.

This scene with its stone figures reminds me of the witch's courtyard in *The Lion, the Witch, and the Wardrobe*. How does Dickens achieve the dark, death-themed description? *Nothing is living. Even the flowers, men, and lions are all made of stone. He mentions a "heavy mass" and "weight"; a Gorgon's head (those who looked upon the Gorgon's snaky head would be turned to stone); a variety of weapons, some of which were used on those he ruled over; and Death is a benefactor. Everything he mentions has a negative effect on the reader.*

Choose a mood you would like to create and then write a paragraph to describe a place. To intensify the mood you're going for, include only things in your description that will add to the mood. Verbs are your friends here. Use specific ones.

Teacher: If you have time in class, you may want to use this as an in-class writing opportunity so students can learn by what their peers have written. If you are teaching a co-op, the paragraph can be due in a week or emailed to you.

Lesson 2

Meet Mr. Dickens

Prisons feature in Dickens' *Tale of Two Cities*, and Dickens knew a thing or two about prisons from first-hand information. So, instead of reading a list of amazingly interesting things about his life, your job is to find out why Dickens knew so much about prisons.

Write your findings here: *Charles Dickens' father was put into debtors' prison when Charles was young. The family lived there, and his father went out daily to work (and work off his debt). Charles was pulled out of school at twelve years of age and put to work in a blacking (shoe polish) factory where he put the blacking into jars and pasted the labels on. He was horrified to suddenly be plunged into this life; and much like H. G. Wells who was pulled from school to work in town, Dickens greatly missed school and his family.*

Lesson 3

Genre and Setting

A Tale of Two Cities is historical fiction.

Backstory

Backstory is the stuff that happens before the story begins. It is mentioned or hinted at so readers know the history of some characters or events. For instance, readers eventually learn the backstory on Madame Defarge, what events shaped her young life and twisted her.

Fun Fact

Students are learning some facts about the guillotine.

If you were to have something named after you, what would you like it to be? *Answers will vary.*

Literary Terms: Theme and Christ Figure

What are the themes in *A Tale of Two Cities*? One can be stated in one word: *resurrection*. Read the subtitle under Book the First. Someone is coming back from the dead, figuratively. This brings up another point. You cannot have a resurrection unless you first have a death. Do not be surprised, then, to see *death, burial,* and *prison* as themes juxtaposed to *resurrection*. They happen literally and figuratively in Dickens' *Tale*.

The **Christ figure** is a type of character that is sacrificed through no fault of his own or who sacrifices himself for the good of others. Obviously, the name is taken from Jesus, who sacrificed himself for us, taking our sins upon himself and bearing our punishment.

Your Novel Notebook

1. Characters—English
2. Characters—French
3. Things that support the idea of "Resurrection" as a theme
4. Things that support "Prison/Death/Burial" as a theme

Additionally, in order to keep track of where you are and which characters you are dealing with, write the **setting of each chapter** (the year and the place) next to each chapter title. Dickens is careful to tell you where you are and in what year so you don't get lost.

If you have not done so already, you may download a free Novel Notebook with the questions already in it by going to http://writingwithsharonwatson.com/ illuminating-literature-when-worlds-collide-gateway/ .

Teacher, here are the characters for your reference, in order of appearance:

1. Jarvis Lorry—a man of business, 70 years old in the beginning of the story

2. Jeremy (Jerry) Cruncher—an "honest tradesman"
3. Lucie Manette—daughter of the old prisoner, 17 years old in the beginning of the story
4. Ernest Defarge—wine shop keeper and Jacques Four
5. Madame Defarge—Monsieur Defarge's wife and the revolutionary spirit embodied
6. Doctor Manette—the old prisoner of 18 years, father to Lucie, 45 years old in the beginning of the story
7. Young Jerry Cruncher—12 years old in the beginning of the story
8. Mrs. Cruncher
9. Charles Darnay—an assumed name, on trial for his life for treason against England for allegedly being in league with France over the American Revolution, 25 years old in the beginning of the story
10. John Barsad—paid spy and witness for the prosecution
11. Roger Cly—former servant of Charles Darnay, paid spy and witness for the prosecution
12. Mr. C. J. Stryver—Solicitor-General, lawyer for Charles Darnay's defense
13. Sydney Carton—a former brilliant law student who currently helps Stryver win his cases
14. Miss Pross—Lucie's old nurse, whom we met unnamed at the Royal George Hotel in Dover
15. Miss Pross's brother Solomon mentioned (see #10)
16. Tall Gaspard—father to the son killed by St. Evrémonde
17. Mender of the roads—reports that he sees a man hanging from the underside of the Marquis' carriage, later becomes part of the Jacquerie
18. Monsieur Gabelle—Evrémonde servant, postmaster, rent collector. His imprisonment at the hands of the French rebels is Darnay's motivation to return to France.
19. "Monseigneur"—unnamed—French aristocracy embodied. Selfish, predatory, "hungry," living in overwhelming luxury in the face of others' extreme famine.
20. Marquis St. Evrémonde—Charles Darnay's uncle. Hard, cold. One of the villains.
21. The Vengeance—unnamed grocer's wife and sidekick to Madame Defarge

Teacher, here is a partial list of elements that support the "Resurrection" theme:
- *"Recalled to Life" (section heading and message on p. 7)*
- *Mr. Lorry was figuratively on his way to dig someone out of a grave. (9)*
- *Lorry's dream (9-11)*
- *"...restore him to life..." (19)*
- *Miss Manette is restored to sensibility at the inn. (19-20)*
- *"The task of recalling him..." (31)*
- *"...a sleeper that moment awake..." (32)*
- *"...which warmed and lighted him..." (34)*
- *"...buried man who had been dug out..." (37)*

- *Darnay is taken from death and prison by Sydney Carton's idea that they look alike. (55-9)*
- *Darnay is acquitted, and Jerry Cruncher refers to the "Recalled to Life" message. (59)*
- *"I hardly seem yet...to belong to this world again." (62)*
- *Sydney Carton leans against a window at the Manette's home, the curtains waving "like spectral wings"—a foreshadowing of his sacrifice hidden in an image. (77)*
- *Resurrection Man (body snatcher) being Jerry Cruncher's night job (125)*
- *"...restoration you have brought to me..."—Dr. Manette to Lucie (125-6)*
- *Seven prisoners released (170)*
- *Roger Cly "feigned death and come to life again!" (236)*
- *Carton remembers "I am the resurrection and the life..." from his father's funeral. (244, 292)*
- *Paris's "glorious sun, rising,...in its long bright rays." (244)*
- *The little seamstress's allusion to Jesus (291)*
- *Lucie and Charles' son Sydney does well in law and is successful, cleansing Sydney Carton's bad name. He, in turn, brings his son Sydney to Paris to tell the story of his parents' struggles and of the original Sydney's sacrifice. (292-3)*

Teacher, here is a partial Prison/Death/Burial list (and page #s):
- *The room at the inn is a "dark room, furnished in a funereal manner...with heavy dark tables." Candles "gloomily reflected...as if they were buried, in deep graves of black mahogany, and no light to speak of could be expected from them until they were dug out." (14)*
- *The mirror in the same room was decorated with "cupids, several headless and all cripples...offering black baskets of Dead Sea fruit to black divinities..." (15)*
- *"I am going to see his Ghost!" (19)*
- *Tellson's Bank is described as small, dark, ugly, and incommodious (like a dungeon). Clients must descend two steps to enter. It has iron bars. It puts people to death upon the slightest provocation, business is carried on gravely, it makes old men out of young. (38-40) It is also described as having perpendicular iron bars, behind which we find Mr. Lorry. (109)*
- *Word picture: "When the Attorney-General ceased, a buzz arose in the court as if a cloud of great blue-flies were swarming about the prisoner, in anticipation of what he was soon to become." (50)*
- *A little boy is run over and killed by the Marquis St. Evrémonde's carriage. (83-4)*
- *The man under the Marquis' carriage (the boy's father) is described as "white as a spectre, tall as a spectre." (88)*
- *The woman in the graveyard wishes for a more permanent headstone than the crudely carved one of wood. (89)*
- *Allusion: The Gorgon turned everything of the Marquis St. Evrémonde to stone, including the Marquis. (90)*

- *The first thing you see when St. Evrémonde enters his chateau is weapons and whips he has used to kill the peasants under his protection in his little town. (90)*
- *"dead darkness" before the assassination (97)*
- *Jerry Cruncher's second "job" as a Resurrection Man or body snatcher (chapter 14)*
- *Seven guards killed at the Bastille. The Bastille itself. (170)*
- *The barriers into Paris were "iron door[s] in a series" to Charles Darnay. (190)*
- *"Cage" and "net" are also used in reference to Darnay's journey from Calais to Paris. (191)*
- *Charles Darnay put into prison. (194-6)*
- *Descriptive words used in the prison: spectral, ghosts all, "ghost of beauty, ghost of stateliness, ghost of elegance...," apparitions. (197-8)*
- *"Now I am left, as if I were dead." (199)*
- *The guillotine itself*
- *A simile: The moon in Paris looked "like a dead face out of the sky." (244)*

Writers' Device: Setup and Payoff

Page 76 contains a story about a prisoner hiding a letter in his cell in England. Please turn to pages 76-7. Read the last paragraph on page 76 and the first paragraph on page 77.

You ask yourself, "What was that all about?" And you won't know until Book the Third. But when you get to that third section and read the event that this little story foreshadowed, you will have an "aha" experience.

Some writers, including screenwriters, call this the **setup** and the **payoff**. The *setup* is the event, conversation, or information that has a meaning as it stands but will be used later in the story. The *payoff* is the event that was foreshadowed by the setup.

Suggested Reading and Homework Plan

Week One:
- ❑ Complete lessons 1-3.
- ❑ Complete lesson 4: Read Book the First (chapters 1-6). Answer questions from this section in your Novel Notebook. If you have not finished the tasks for Week One yet, do so now.

Week Two: Lesson 5
- ❑ Read Book the Second (chapters 1-24) in the middle of the book. Answer questions from this section in your Novel Notebook.

Week Three: Lesson 6
- ❑ Read Book the Third (chapters 1-15) at the end of the book. Answer questions from this section in your Novel Notebook.

Week Four:
- ❑ Choose your activity (see the end of the chapter) and begin work on it.
- ❑ Complete lessons 7-8.
- ❑ Complete your activity. Your teacher will tell you when this is due.

Lesson 4

Stuff You Might Want to Know + Chapter Questions

Teacher, students are learning things chapter by chapter that will help them understand what they are reading. They are also answering questions in their Novel Notebooks. Not all chapters have questions.

Here's the link to download free Novel Notebooks: http://writingwithsharonwatson.com/illuminating-literature-when-worlds-collide-gateway/ .

Book the First: Recalled to Life
Chapter 3—Questions
1. At one of the taverns, what does Jerry call himself? *An honest tradesman (p. 9)*
2. How old is the emaciated man in Jarvis Lorry's dreams? *45 years old (p. 10)*

Chapter 4
Mr. Lorry and Lucie are traveling across the English Channel from Dover to Calais (Kal-AY). Find these towns on a map.

Chapter 5
1. There are two personifications/anthropomorphisms (giving inanimate objects/ideas human characteristics) on page 22. What are they? *The neighborhood of St. Antoine and Hunger.*
2. What is the signal by which Madame Defarge warns her husband of newcomers to the wine shop? *Toothpick, grain of a cough, and slightly upraised eyebrow (p. 24)*
3. What is Monsieur Defarge's relationship with the old prisoner? *Defarge was the doctor's young servant. (p. 26)*
4. Why were the three men and the wine-shop keeper calling each other Jacques? *It was a code word for the men who were on the inside track of the resistance movement. (p. 25)*
5. What does Doctor Manette keep in the dirty pouch at his neck? *A few hairs from his wife's head; he found these upon his sleeve when he was secretly arrested. (p. 33)*

Lesson 5

Teacher, this is a week-long lesson and has the most chapters from *A Tale of Two Cities* in it. Students are advised to pace themselves.

Book the Second: The Golden Thread
Chapter 1—Questions
1. Why is Jerry Cruncher against his wife's praying? *He believes she is praying against his success and prosperity. (p. 41)*
2. List the clues to Jerry Cruncher's real night work, even though he calls himself an "honest tradesman." *Clay-covered boots (41), red-eyed and grim as if up all night (42), rusty fingers (43)*

Chapter 3
1. How does the lawyer for the defense (the Solicitor-General) show the reader that John Barsad might be a scoundrel? *By asking him if he had ever been in prison, been kicked down the stairs, had cheated at cards, and so forth. (p. 50)*
2. What information does the Solicitor-General (Mr. Stryver) draw out of Roger Cly to show that Roger might be a scoundrel, too? *By asking him if he had ever stolen that silver teapot and the mustard pot, showing that there had been trouble with him before and that he might not be the model citizen the court described. (p. 51)*

Chapter 4
1. Book the Second is subtitled "The Golden Thread." In Chapter 4, we find out what that means. Who or what is that golden thread and what is linked by it? *Lucie, who by her love and concern, link the past and the present (healing her father of his incoherence and fear). (p. 60)*

Chapter 5
1. How does Stryver use Sydney Carton? *He uses Carton's superior brains by showing Carton the cases he's working on and asking how he can win it. He also pays Carton to help him, in addition to giving him all the liquor he wants. (pp. 65, 67)*

Chapter 7
1. Describe Monsieur the Marquis by his looks and actions. His actions in this chapter have far-reaching consequences for himself and for others in this novel. *His nose is "slightly pinched at the top of each nostril." He is treacherous and cruel, drives with "furious recklessness" through the crowded town, with "an inhuman abandonment of consideration." He runs over a little boy, calls the people rats and dogs, throws money at them as if to make up for the death, and wishes to exterminate them from the earth. (pp. 83-5)*

Chapter 9
1. What is your reaction when you learn that Marquis St. Evrémonde's awaited nephew is Charles Darnay? *Answers will vary.*

2. What is the alliteration Dickens uses on page 95? (Alliteration is repeating the first sounds of words.) Why is the repetition of that particular sound a fitting one in this case? *"...cruelly, craftily, and closely compressed." The "K" sounds make it sound hard and harsh.*

3. What is Charles's mother's dying wish? *"...to have mercy and to redress." That is, to right a wrong. (p. 94)*

4. Whom, figuratively, did the Gorgon turn to stone? *The Marquis St. Évrémonde, Charles Darnay's uncle. (p. 98)*

5. Who is this Jacques? *Jacques is the code name for the men in the resistance at the wine shop, but specifically, this Jacques is the dead boy's father. (p. 99)*

6. Did Charles kill his uncle? *You may be tempted to think so, but no, he did not.*

Chapter 10

1. What is Charles Darnay's profession? *He teaches French literature and language. (p. 99)*

2. What are the two promises? *(1) That if Lucie should speak of Darnay, Dr. Manette will not be negative about him, and (2) that if Lucie and Darnay marry, on their wedding day Darnay will reveal to the doctor who Darnay really is. (p. 104)*

3. Why does Dr. Manette stop Charles twice? *He suspects who Charles really is, and he doesn't want to know. (p. 104)*

4. How does the reader know that Dr. Manette is upset without Dickens' writing, "Dr. Manette was upset"? Incidentally, the last four paragraphs of this chapter are a fine example of the writer's device "Show, Don't Tell." Dickens shows actions and reactions instead of telling the reader the obvious. *Lucie's reaction tells us that something is wrong, and then we see the doctor back at the cobbler's bench, a place he goes only when troubled. (p. 105)*

Chapter 11

1. In what way does Mr. Lorry divide himself up into two people? *He calls himself a "man of business" and an "old fellow" who used to carry Lucie around as a little girl. (p. 111)*

Chapter 13

1. Do you believe the dissipated Sydney Carton when he says he'd do anything for Lucie and for those she loves? *Answers will vary.*

Chapter 14

1. Look on your character list. Who is Roger Cly? *One of the corrupt Old Bailey spies who had testified against Charles Darnay.*

2. What are this "honest tradesman's" tools? *Sack, crowbar, rope, and chain. (p. 122)*

3. What is a Resurrection Man? *A body snatcher, one who digs up people to sell to the medical profession for experiments or for medical students or to steal anything of value that was buried with the dead.*

4. Dickens uses "Show, Don't Tell" again with respect to Jerry Cruncher's lack of success in the night. What are the clues that tell you that Jerry was unsuccessful? *He beat his wife, he is angry, and he eats little breakfast. (pp. 124-5)*

Chapter 15
1. The mender of roads, whom you met in Chapter 8, has become a member of Defarge's fraternity. What was the clue? *He is now called Jacques. (p. 127)*
2. What decision do the four Jacques come to? *They agree to destroy the St. Evrémonde chateau and any family members left alive. (p. 132)*
3. What is the "register" the Jacques talk about? *The piece of cloth that Madame Defarge has been knitting. She somehow manages to knit into the material the name or a code for the name of anyone she thinks should die. (p. 132)*
4. What crime had the tall father of the dead child committed that he should be hanged so? *He had stabbed the Marquis to death. (p. 131)*

Chapter 16
1. Check your character list. Where have you seen John Barsad before? *He was one of the corrupt Old Bailey spies who testified against Charles Darnay. Now he's a spy in Paris. (p. 136)*
2. What crucial information does Barsad the spy tell the Defarges? *The man who is to marry Lucie is the nephew of the hated Marquis. (p. 142)*

Chapter 21
1. What is the significance of "One Hundred and Five, North Tower"? *That is the room number and the tower where Dr. Manette was unjustly and secretly imprisoned for 18 years.*

Chapter 24
1. What does Stryver call the "unknown" nephew Evrémonde? *A scoundrel and a coward. (p. 185)*
2. From where is Gabelle writing? *A prison cell in France. (p. 186)*
3. What is his crime? *"Treason against the majesty of the people" by being a representative of an emigrant (Charles Darnay). (p. 187)*
4. Why does Charles finally decide to go to France? *He feels it is his duty to help an old family servant, even if he never used him. (pp. 187-9)*

Lesson 6

Teacher, this is a week-long lesson. Students are advised to pace themselves.

Book the Third
Chapter 3
Why do you think that in literature (as in life), evil seems stronger and more powerful than good?

1. *It is easier to portray evil than good.*
2. *Good becomes brighter against a backdrop of evil. If a teenage girl tutors young students in the inner city at a homeless shelter, readers would view that as good. But if she is attacked because she is not of the same race as the students, she is taunted because she lives in a nice home, her tires are slashed, and she is shown disrespect even by her students because they mistrust her, then her goodness takes on heroic proportions. She is suddenly seen by readers as "more good" because of the difficult opposition she bears up under.*
3. *If the evil is really strong, then it is a powerful victory when the good triumphs—the wickedness of the antagonist can serve to define the goodness of the protagonist when the protagonist eventually wins. Think of superheroes. Their enemies are truly wicked, perverted, strong, and cunning. What kind of superhero would the protagonist be if his enemies were weak, sniveling wimps?*
4. *On page 286, Dickens assures the reader that "love [is] always so much stronger than hate."*

Chapter 4
1. There is a definite change in Dr. Manette in Book the Third. He is stronger, more sure of himself and his abilities, more assertive, and less fearful of losing his sanity. What brought about the change? Find the sentence on page 210 that explains his metamorphosis. *"For the first time the doctor felt, now, that his suffering was strength and power."*

Chapter 5
1. Who do you think has just come to visit Mr. Lorry? *It is Sydney Carton.*

Chapter 6
1. Of what crime is Charles Darnay accused? *The crime of being an emigrant. At that time, anyone who left France to live elsewhere was considered a traitor, even if they had left years ago. (p. 219)*
2. At his "trial," what are the points in his favor?
    - *He had relinquished his title.*
    - *He had married not an Englishwoman but a French woman.*
    - *He had supported himself rather than live off the French people.*
    - *He had returned to help a former family servant.*
    - *He had been tried in England as a traitor to that country, concerning the American Revolution and France's participation in it.*
    - *He had befriended Dr. Manette, who was popular due to his history.*

Chapter 8
1. When Miss Pross finds her brother Solomon in a wine shop in Paris, he is not happy to be found. Refer to your list of characters to remember who John Barsad was originally. What trouble did he get someone into? *He was a spy for the English gaolers who testified against Charles Darnay falsely.*

2. You will remember the night that Jerry Cruncher, as a Resurrection Man, had been unsuccessful (pp. 124-5). He had even beaten his wife, suspecting her of praying against his success. Now you know why he was so upset. The information he reveals in this chapter is the payoff. What did he know? *There was no body in Roger Cly's coffin. Roger Cly was still alive. (p. 236)*

Chapter 9

1. Jerry Cruncher seeks to make amends with Mr. Lorry by offering to do what? *He promises to become a gravedigger, to put people into the ground, not dig them out. (p. 239)*
2. What deal has Sydney Carton made with John Barsad/Solomon Pross? *As a spy, John/Solomon has access to the prison and can go anywhere. Sydney, through John/Solomon, makes sure he can gain access to Charles Darnay once, if things go bad. (p. 239)*
3. The people, through violence, have become as hard and unfeeling as their former rulers. Find the sentence that best sums this up. *"If the Republic should demand of you the sacrifice of your child herself, you would have no duty but to sacrifice her." (p. 247)*

Chapter 10

1. In what way did Dr. Manette "denounce" Charles Darnay? (This is the payoff from pages 76 and 168-9.) *When he was 10 years into his prison sentence, he wrote a letter that told the story of the two St. Evrémonde brothers and their cruelty and treacherousness. He denounced them and their descendants in this letter. (p. 258)*
2. In this chapter, we learn who sent Dr. Manette to prison so long ago. Who was it and what crimes was the man trying to hide? *The Marquis St. Evrémonde, who had raped a young wife in his neighborhood and killed her husband through hard labor.*
3. We also learn what Charles' mother charged him to do when he grew up. What was that mission? *He was charged to find the younger sister of the now dead wife, in order to show her compassion by giving her the money gained by selling his mother's jewels. (p. 257)*

Chapter 11

1. We finally learn why Charles Darnay often went to France earlier. (Remember that going to France was the reason he was put on trial as a traitor to England when we first met him.) What has he been doing all this time in France? *Trying to find the younger sister of the wronged wife. (p. 260)*

Chapter 12

1. What is Madame Defarge's secret? *She is the younger sister. (p. 264)*

Chapter 14

1. What are Jerry Cruncher's two vows? *Never to body snatch again and never to interfere with his wife's praying again. (p. 283)*

Chapter 15
Questions
1. What number is Sydney Carton? *Twenty-three. (p. 292)*
2. Write the future fate of these people:

- John Barsad and Roger Cly: *dead by the guillotine*
- Ernest Defarge: *dead by the guillotine*
- Lucie Manette Darnay: *has another son and names him Sydney; remembers the date of Sydney Carton's sacrifice by weeping; honors her husband*
- Dr. Manette: *in his right mind, a good doctor*
- Mr. Lorry: *eventually dies and makes Lucie and Charles his heirs*
- Charles Darnay: *honors Sydney Carton, continues to love his wife*
- Sydney Darnay (Lucie and Charles' son): *excels in his profession and becomes a judge; has a child named Sydney and takes him to the former site of the guillotine to tell the boy the story of his parents' ordeal and of the original Sydney's sacrifice.*

After You've Read the Book

Lesson 7

Five-Star Report

Students are filling out a graph to show how they felt about *A Tale of Two Cities*. 1 = Couldn't stand it. 5 = Loved it!

Reward: Distribute the small reward to each student who finished reading *A Tale of Two Cities*, perhaps candy in a carton to tie in to Sydney Carton's sacrificial death.

Colliding Worlds

Below are a few suggestions. Students may have others.
1. The common people versus the ruling class
2. *Vengeance and retribution versus mercy and forgiveness*
3. *Death versus life*
4. *Peace versus anarchy*
5. *A person's ability to do evil versus his ability to do good*

Which of these colliding worlds have you experienced in your life? *Answers will vary.*

Complete the Online Quizzes and Survey

Teacher, students are instructed to go to http://WritingWithSharonWatson.com/ illuminating-literature-when-worlds-collide-gateway/ to get links to complete the following:
- "Yes, I read it" quiz—graded online for you

- Literary Terms Quiz (themes, setup and payoff, backstory, prolepsis [flashforward], literary elements, and Christ figure)—graded online for you
- Opinion Survey—no grade, but answers to the opinion questions may help you develop a strategy for your discussion time.

Students are allowed two attempts to complete the quizzes and one for the opinion survey. Also, the quiz site will email a full report of the quiz (questions, answers, the correct answers, and grade) to the email address your student signed in with.

Password for quizzes and survey: DICKENS

Teacher, if you prefer a paper quizzes, you'll find them in *Illuminating Literature: When Worlds Collide, Quizzes and Answer Manual,* available for sale at http://writingwithsharonwatson.com/illuminating-literature-when-worlds-collide.

Opinion questions have no correct answer; students are graded on participation. Their answers to the opinion questions may help you develop a strategy for your discussion time.

Vocabulary Quizzola for *A Tale of Two Cities*

Objectives:
- To reinforce good vocabulary habits and awareness.
- To gain a grade, which is separate from the Grading Grid.

Directions: Match the definition on the right with the correct word on the left by entering the letter in the correct blank. Numbers after the words indicate page numbers in the Dover Thrift version for this course of *A Tale of Two Cities* where the words occur. **Ask your teacher if this is an open-book quiz.** Correct answers are worth 5 points each.

_D_1. immolate, 49	A. talking a lot and loudly
_F_2. pernicious, 49	B. quench
_K_3. timorous, 52	C. thieves
_N_4. commiseration, 57	D. sacrifice
_I_5. strait, 63	E. made saintly
_T_6. trebly, 72	F. wicked
_C_7. footpads, 78	G. ending
_H_8. patrician, 83	H. aristocratic
_A_9. vociferating, 119	I. difficulty
_R_10. inundation, 167	J. warning bells
_L_11. tumult, 167	K. shy, timid
_E_12. beatified, 175	L. noise
_S_13. kine, 177	M. subterfuge, trickery
_J_14. tocsin, 178	N. sympathy
_P_15. razed, 186	O. low carts used for hauling dung
_Q_16. awry, 203	P. flattened

_O_ 17. tumbrils, 213
_B_ 18. slake, 213
_M_ 19. tergiversation, 234
_G_ 20. cessation, 250

Q. wrong or crooked
R. flood
S. cows
T. three times as much

Vertical words hidden in correct answers: KNIT and CHARLES
Grade: _____

Send the Manuscript Back!

It is interesting to note that Dickens did not have Lucie Darnay and Madame Defarge face off as equals in the end. Perhaps it would have sullied a Victorian heroine's reputation to shoot, even accidentally, her mortal enemy. Perhaps the heroine in Dickens' time had to be passive in order to be good. Whatever the case, the resolution would not fly with today's editors. The main protagonist has to win over the main antagonist. She cannot send her old nurse to do the dirty work for her. Good has to meet evil—and gain some sort of victory. Be aware of this when you write your own masterpiece!

Teacher, students may rewrite the conflict between Miss Pross and Madame Defarge in their Novel Notebooks. You may also want to discuss a new encounter here.

A Motif

One interesting motif that emerges in this story is one of doubles. Consider the above list of doubles, and, in one complete sentence, write what you think Dickens was trying to say about people: *Possible answers: (1) Within each person is the capacity for great good or great evil, or (2) Each person is a complex repository of personality traits and actions, (3) Humanity possesses the potential for great good or great evil, or (4) Sometimes we are the best of people* and *the worst of people.*

Lesson 8

Questions for Discussion

Teacher, before delving into the discussion questions, grease the wheels with these questions:

1. What questions do you have about *A Tale of Two Cities*?
2. What aspects of this book appealed to you?
3. What is your impression of this book?

These preliminary questions will help to clear up any misunderstandings or miscomprehensions from the books, and they'll get students talking during the discussion session because they are open-ended questions. Students can answer other students' questions, too. This pre-discussion time may also serve to answer some of the questions printed below or can be a springboard to any of the aspects of the book you want to focus on.

You now have a lengthy list of events, dialogue, descriptions, and so forth, to support the Resurrection theme and the Prison/Death/Burial theme. Share these with your teacher or discuss them with friends or classmates.

As a reminder, Romans 12:19 (NIV): Do not take revenge, my dear friends, but leave room for God's wrath, for it is written: "It is mine to avenge; I will repay," says the Lord.

1. How did each of these characters below handle the wrongs done to them? Which method seems the most worthy to you? Which method is reflected in what you read in Scripture? This questions corresponds with the vengeance/forgiveness theme.
   - Dr. Manette
   - Lucie Manette Darnay
   - Charles Darnay
   - Madam Thérèse Defarge
   - Gaspard
   - Gabelle, the Evrémonde's representative in town
   - The young seamstress in the timbrell

   o Dr. Manette—*unjustly imprisoned for 18 years; done "in secret" so that no one knew where he was or what had happened. After being found and rescued, he spent much time cobbling and then concentrated on Lucie. When he found out that Charles was the nephew of the man who sent him to prison, he bravely dealt with the information, even though it cost him nine days of sanity. He did not hold it against Charles, nor did he tell Lucie. When he returned to France, he doctored anyone who needed his help.*
   o Charles Darnay—*falsely accused of being an English traitor for the American colonists during their revolution. Years later, he was put into prison in France with an illegal law for being an emigrant. He was acquitted and then imprisoned again as being the son of a Marquis. He loved Lucie and her father, even though they gave evidence against him at his first trial. He tried to protect them when he secretly left for France. Carton was so sure of Darnay's sense of self-sacrifice that Carton bought chemicals to knock Darnay out at the critical point in the prison switcheroo. Though wronged many times, he still tries to right old wrongs perpetrated by others.*
   o Lucie Manette Darnay—*spends her energies on restoring her father instead of hating or trying to get even with his enemies. She accepts and cares for the dissipated Carton. Instead of fighting the violent peasants, she concentrates on making a home for her father and daughter, visiting a spot on the pavement where her imprisoned husband might see her. She also appeals to Madame*

Defarge's sense of the sisterhood of women and to her sense of mercy instead of threatening her.

- o The tall father of the boy killed by the Marquis St. Evrémonde—*takes his revenge on the Marquis by stabbing him in his chateau later that night.*

- o Madame Defarge—*spirited away as a young girl to safety after the Marquis St. Evrémonde had raped her older sister and killed her sister's husband and after the Marquis' brother had killed her brother. She is also one of the many of the middle and lower classes who has had to sit quietly by as the upper classes run them into the ground by taking exorbitant taxes, by refusing them justice and mercy and compassion, by treating them as rats to be exterminated. Every day, she sees extreme poverty, famine, dying children, mistreated men and women, unjustly imprisoned people, and punishments out of proportion to the crimes. She reacts by planning her own vengeance, by becoming just as hard and cold as her oppressors are, and by keeping a knitted register of those she is going to exterminate.*

2. If you aren't supposed to take revenge, what else can you do? *Answers will vary.*

3. In one complete sentence, sum up this vengeance/forgiveness theme (in other words, what Dickens might have been saying about vengeance and forgiveness). *Possible answers: (1) Forgiveness is better and lasts longer than vengeance, or (2) Forgiveness results in life while vengeance results in death.*

4. Of all the people who have been wronged in this story, with whom do you have the most sympathy? Explain. *Answers will vary.*

5. Do you think Madame Defarge's anger and cruelty are justified in the light of her family's fate? Explain. *Answers will vary.*

6. Which is the most memorable character to you? Explain. *Answers will vary.*

7. Why does evil seem so much more powerful than good in literature and in life?
   - *It is easier to portray evil than good.*
   - *Good becomes brighter against a backdrop of evil. If a teenage girl tutors young students in the inner city at a homeless shelter, readers would view that as good. But if she is attacked because she is not of the same race as the students, she is taunted because she lives in a nice home, her tires are slashed, and she is shown disrespect even by her students because they mistrust her, then her goodness takes on heroic proportions. She is suddenly seen by readers as "more good" because of the difficult opposition she bears up under.*
   - *If the evil is really strong, then it is a powerful victory when the good triumphs—the wickedness of the antagonist can serve to define the goodness of the protagonist when the protagonist eventually wins. Think of superheroes. Their enemies are truly wicked, perverted, strong, and cunning. What kind of superhero would the protagonist be if his enemies were weak, sniveling wimps?*
   - *On page 286, Dickens assures the reader that "love [is] always so much stronger than hate."*
   - *In life, we don't always see the endings, as we do in literature.*
   - *In life, evil can only destroy, but good builds, heals, encourages, saves, rescues, and so on.*

If You Liked This Book

Students are reading and adding titles of books similar to *A Tale of Two Cities* in theme or genre.

This is the end of lesson 8.

Your Choice of Activities

Note: Choose only one of the following activities. Read all of them carefully before you make your decision. Below you will find a short explanation of each activity. Your teacher will tell you when this is due.

- Be the Author—Write a short story.
- Be the Author II—Write a different ending to the novel.
- History Buff—Compare and contrast the American Revolution with the French Revolution.
- History Buff II—Find out all the interesting stuff that came out of the French Revolution (like the metric system and encyclopedias). Or research Dr. Guillotin or the Bastille.
- The Artist in You—Draw, paint, sculpt, or create a mural.
- Be the Prisoner—Live for one day as Charles Darnay did.
- Interview—Interview a prisoner of war.
- Be the Cartographer—Make a map.
- Be the Thespian—Act out a scene.
- Be the Musician—Write a song.

Be the Author

Something in the book might have sparked your imagination. Maybe you have some ideas of your own concerning the same themes Dickens wrote about. Write your own short story or poem in response to *A Tale of Two Cities*.

Be the Author II

As mentioned earlier, no writer today could get away with pitting a minor character like Miss Pross against a major antagonist like Madame Defarge in a climactic scene. Rewrite the scene where Madame Defarge comes looking for Lucie and her daughter. Make Lucie be an active participant in her own search for happiness, safety, and the safety of the ones she loves.

History Buff

There are many similarities between the American Revolution and the French Revolution. For instance, did you know that Thomas Paine, the supporter of the American Revolution who wrote *Common Sense*, also wrote pamphlets for the French Revolution?

142

Despite the similarities, the two revolutions are characterized quite differently in history and by historians. Research the differences between the two.

When you have finished your research, create a chart showing the comparisons and the contrasts between the two revolutions.

History Buff II

Did you know that the metric system did not exist until rebels in the French Revolution developed it? The men and women of that time were so intent on overturning and rebelling against everything familiar in their government, society, and religion, that they changed or invented many things during this time.

Find out all the interesting stuff that came out of the French Revolution and make a list.

The Artist in You

There are many dramatic scenes in *A Tale of Two Cities*. Draw, paint, sculpt, create a mural, or use another medium to depict a scene, a character, a mood, or a theme contained there. Show your results to a teacher or an interested viewer.

Be the Prisoner

When Charles Darnay is thrown into prison the first time in France, he paces off the measurements of his cell: five paces by four and a half paces. That's all the space he has to live in. Measure out this same area somewhere in your home, mark your boundaries, and live there for one day. Record your reactions and any events, and then report to your teacher or to fellow students.

Interview

There are many veterans from WWII, the Korean War, Viet Nam, Desert Storm, and other wars and conflicts. Some of these men and women were prisoners of war (POWs). Ask for an interview with a POW and listen to the stories. Record the interview, if possible, or take notes. Then write up what you learn, weaving his or her stories into one narrative. Share your results with your teacher or fellow students.

Be the Cartographer

Create a map of the two cities in this novel. Include the English Channel, London, Dover, Calais, Paris, and the neighborhood of St. Antoine (you will need a detailed map of Paris for this).

Be the Thespian

There are many dramatic scenes in this tale. Find other actors, rewrite the scene for the stage, and act out the scene in front of a live audience. Include costumes and scenery, if possible.

Be the Musician

Victor Hugo's *Les Misérables* has been made into a musical, so why not *A Tale of Two Cities*? Write a song about a tense moment or a favorite character and then perform it. Check out this song inspired by the infamous Madame Defarge: http://wn.com/madame_defarge

(You'll have to look at the playlist on the right side of that page and select "Madame Defarge" with the guitarists.)

Teacher, your grading grid for *A Tale of Two Cities* is on the next page. The grid is marked for a possible 100 points per book. Please feel free to adjust it to your needs and expectations. You have permission to copy it as many times as needed for your own class, co-op, reading group, book-of-the-month club, or family.

Grading Grid for *A Tale of Two Cities*

Student's Name: _____

Online "Yes, I read it" quiz, graded online. 1-10 points	
Online literary terms quiz, graded online. 1-10 points	
Participation in opinion questions online. 1-10 points	
Quality of participation in discussions. 1-20 points	
Successful completion of lessons and assignments. 1-20 points	
Successful completion of activity. 1-10 points	
Finished reading the book. 1-20 points.	
Total grade for *A Tale of Two Cities*	

Writing with *Sharon Watson*

Chapter 7: *Fahrenheit 451*

Simon & Schuster   ISBN: 978-1-4516-7331-9

Facebook Posts

If your group or co-op meets monthly, you may want to keep in touch with the students and keep them interested in the novels by creating a secret Facebook group for only them and their parents. Feel free to devise your own questions or find your own links to interesting material.

- Watch Ray Bradbury reveal interesting things in his own words on video in his own home: http://www.raybradbury.com/at_home_clips.html#. When you get there, click on "Bradbury on Fahrenheit 451." Then come back and tell us what you think about his ideas.
- Watch this interview with Bradbury as he explains some fun facts about *Fahrenheit 451* and how he came to write it: https://www.youtube.com/watch?v=FL_y6gtxLvQ. He says he was enraged about his encounter with the policeman, and this is what made him write the precursor of *Fahrenheit 451*, "The Pedestrian." If you were to write a short story about something that really enrages (or peeves) you, what would it be?
- Do you suffer from FOMO? FOMO is "fear of missing out" and has been around for ages, in different forms. Watch this YouTube video about it: https://www.youtube.com/watch?v=KqgaJx5X18Q. How long do you think you could go without looking at your mobile device or tablet? How do you feel when it is unavailable to you?
- "No, no, it's not books at all you're looking for . . . ," says Professor Faber. It's not the *books*; it's what's *in* them. Where do you find your awareness of life, your knowledge and wisdom?
- Bradbury posits that we lose something important in life if we are constantly interacting with our technology and rely on our technology and sound bites and "Seashell thimbles" (a constant stream from our earbuds) but don't take the time to think, imagine, plan, weigh alternatives, meditate, form opinions, talk with others, engage with others intellectually, philosophize, read, have downtime, enjoy the simple things in life, and so on.

  C. S. Lewis (our next author) says it this way: "We live, in fact, in a world starved for solitude, silence, and private: and therefore starved for meditation and true friendship." What can you do to carve out more time in your life for silence, meditation, and friendship?

- Catch this fun summation of *Fahrenheit 451*: https://www.youtube.com/watch?v=kjCk8J6L_SI. Other than the guy's energy, what leaps out at you?

- John of the vlogbrothers asks these questions in that video: "When do you feel *least* like you're wasting your life?" and "When do you feel most alive?" What do you say?
- What question would you like to ask Ray Bradbury?

Before You Read the Book

Lesson 1

Suggested Reading and Homework Plan: Preview

Week One:
☐ Complete lessons 1-3.
Week Two:
☐ Read "The Hearth and the Salamander" in *Fahrenheit 451.*
Week Three:
☐ Read "The Sieve and the Sand" and "Burning Bright" in *Fahrenheit 451.*
Week Four:
☐ Choose your activity (see the end of the chapter) and begin work on it.
☐ Complete lessons 4-9.
☐ There's no Vocabulary Quizzola this month! Woo-hoo!
☐ Complete your activity. Your teacher will tell you when this is due.

Imitate!

Find the paragraph in *Fahrenheit 451* that begins and ends with this: "The Mechanical Hound slept but did not sleep, . . . its eight legs spidered under it on rubber-padded paws." If you are using the 2012 Simon & Schuster Paperback edition of the book, you'll find the paragraph on pages 21-22.

Read the paragraph and then fill in the following list of wonderful imagery Bradbury uses to introduce you to this Hound.

Visual imagery (sight): *softly illuminated, dark corner, dim light, moonlight, light flickered, ruby glass, brass, copper, steel.*
Olfactory imagery (smell): *None.*
Auditory imagery (sound): *humming.*
Tactile imagery (touch, what it feels like to the skin): *nylon-brushed nostrils, rubber-padded paws.*
Kinetic imagery (movement): *vibrating, faintly trembling, quivered gently.*

Boring paragraphs. We all know some. They are like black and white pictures that should be in vibrant color. Read the dull paragraphs below and **change them any way you like.** Change the whole narrative or focus in on one or two experiences. Be sure to include lots of **sensory imagery** (sight, scent, taste, movement, and so forth) and **vivid verbs**. Make readers feel as though they are there. Here you go:

> Chris and I went to this amusement park yesterday, and it was a lot of fun. We couldn't decide on which ride to ride first, so we closed our eyes, spun around, and then opened our eyes. Chris was looking at the Tilt-O-Stomach, and I was looking at the Savage Beast rollercoaster. We decided we would ride those two rides first.
>
> On the way to the Tilt-O-Stomach, we ate chili dogs and drank two sodas each. Well, I almost did, anyway. A clown came out of a doorway and scared me. I jumped and dropped my first soda and had to buy another one.
>
> Chris's ride was fun. It went around fast and then tilted us. It was so fast that we stuck to the inside of it. We tried to pull our legs and arms from the side of the ride, but they were stuck. Even our heads were hard to move. At one point, my stomach didn't feel very good.
>
> Next, we rode the Savage Beast rollercoaster. It was fun. When we got off the ride, we were dizzy. It was hard to walk straight. We walked into this thing that was spraying people with water as they walked by. It felt good because we were hot.
>
> We had a good time. I think we'll go again tomorrow.

Teacher: If you have time in class, you may want to use this as an in-class writing opportunity so students can learn by what their peers have written. If you are teaching a co-op, the paragraph can be due in a week or emailed to you. I think you'll be amazed and amused at the variety and inventiveness of your students!

Lesson 2

Meet Mr. Bradbury

Teacher, students are reading about Bradbury's life.

Write two things about Bradbury's life that surprise or interest you. *Answers will vary.*

Lesson 3

Fun Fact

Students are learning about how the story of *Fahrenheit 451* first came about.

   If you want to hear more about *Fahrenheit 451* and other interesting things about Ray Bradbury in his own words on video in his own home, go to www.raybradbury.com/at_home_clips.html# and be prepared for a treat.

Genre

Fahrenheit 451 is a futuristic story in the science-fiction (sci-fi) genre. Watch this interview with Bradbury as he explains some fun facts about *Fahrenheit 451* and how he came to write it: https://www.youtube.com/watch?v=FL_y6gtxLvQ.

If the Garden of Eden is an example of heaven on earth (**utopia**), what is an example of **dystopia**? Write your answer below: *Answers will vary.*

The Man's Got Style

Students are learning about **style, loose or cumulative sentences**, and **periodic sentences.**

Publication Date and Setting

In what year was *Fahrenheit 451* first published? *1953*

Please read page 1 through the top of page 5 and answer the questions below:
1. At what time of day does this story begin? *Midnight*
2. At what time of year? *Fall*
3. In what time period? *In the future*
4. Although there is no name, in what kind of place is the story happening? *In an American city and suburb*

Your Novel Notebook

Teacher, this is what students are casually looking for or marking in their novels. However, it is not required for them to record these in their Novel Notebooks:
1. Anything to support the theme of censorship (but be looking for something hidden behind this theme that's more powerful)
2. Anything to support the theme of ignorance versus knowledge
3. Mirrors and moonlight imagery
4. Animal and nature imagery
5. References or allusions to Christian stories or phrases
6. Paradoxes (statements that seem untrue because they contradict themselves. Examples: Jesus is seen in the Bible as both a servant and a king. In *Fahrenheit 451*, the Mechanical Hound is described as alive but not alive.)

Students will be turning off all technology—mobiles, tablets, TVs, radios, social media, and so forth—for a time period of their choosing. Then they'll record the results of their experiment in their Novel Notebook.

To download a free Novel Notebook with the questions already in it, go to http://writingwithsharonwatson.com/illuminating-literature-when-worlds-collide-gateway/ .

A Warning

There is swearing in this book.

Suggested Reading and Homework Plan

Week One:

- ❏ Complete lessons 1-3. If you have not completed your tasks for this week, complete them now.

Week Two:

- ❏ Read "The Hearth and the Salamander" in *Fahrenheit 451*.

Week Three:

- ❏ Read "The Sieve and the Sand" and "Burning Bright" in Fahrenheit 451.

Week Four:

- ❏ Choose your activity (see the end of the chapter) and begin work on it.
- ❏ Complete lessons 4-9.
- ❏ There's no Vocabulary Quizzola this month! Woo-hoo!
- ❏ Complete your activity. Your teacher will tell you when this is due.

After You've Read the Book

Lesson 4

Five-Star Report

Students are filling out a graph to show how they felt about *Fahrenheit 451*. 1 = Couldn't stand it. 5 = Loved it!

Teacher, the reward can be Twizzlers (strawberry flavored) to represent Clarisse or Red Hots to represent fire.

Colliding Worlds

What worlds are colliding with each other? *Your students may think of others.*

1. *Book burners versus book lovers*
2. *Ignorance versus knowledge*
3. *Technology versus nature*
4. *Fast-paced modern life versus time for contemplation*
5. *Government versus its people*

What does it mean that Bradbury pits book burners against book lovers? How is the conflict between book burners and book lovers resolved? *It means he is pitting ignorance against knowledge, that he is showing the value of taking time to think and enjoy nature rather than be a destroyer and be caught up in activities that sear the soul. The conflict between book burners versus book lovers is resolved when the bombs fall on the city. In other words, the book burners have themselves been burned up; their lives were ruined because they did not engage in any public discourse about their country or their civilization or try to effect a change.*

As a result of the conflicts Montag experiences, what negative things happen in his life? Write your answer below: *He loses his wife, his job, his house, his reputation, his friends, his sense of safety. He kills his boss. He is a hunted, haunted man.*

What positive things happen as a result of the conflicts Montag experiences? Write your answer here: *He gains an understanding of the importance of thinking and having time to think, to process information and make important decisions based on what he's thought about. He gains friends who value books and the things in them. He feels more at peace with himself. He belongs to a group of men who are equipped to rebuild society.*

Lesson 5

Literary Element: Plot

What do we learn about Montage and the setting in the normalcy phase of *Fahrenheit 451?* Write your answer here: *Montage is a fireman who lives in a suburb. He loves his job and is coming home at midnight at the end of his shift. Through his conversation with Clarisse, we learn he is subconsciously unhappy. He is married. His wife tried to commit suicide. We are in the future, where it is considered unusual for anyone to be out walking at night for pleasure.*

What is the inciting incident in *Fahrenheit 451? Clarisse asks Montag, "Are you happy?" and that gets him thinking, as does his wife's attempted suicide. But Montag takes action and enters his story when he steals a book at the old woman's house.*

What are some major mountain peaks or crises in which Montag finds himself?
1. Mildred finds Montag's book under his pillow, and Beatty suspects something.
2. *Beatty and the Mechanical Hound are at Montag's front door at different times.*
3. *The harrowing subway ride provides a crisis in Montag's life—will he continue on or return home to burn the book?*
4. *Montag reads a poem to Mildred's friends, any one of which could turn him in.*
5. *The firemen report to Montag's house in order to burn it. Montag is ordered to burn his own house.*
6. *He must decide what to do after he burns his house. He must escape Beatty and the Mechanical Hound. He kills Beatty.*
7. *He encounters the Mechanical Hound.*
8. *He must decide whether to go to Faber's house and what to do after that encounter.*
9. *He must decide whether to approach the men at the outdoor fire.*

Do "The Hearth and the Salamander" and "The Sand and the Sieve" end in the middle of a crisis?
"The Hearth and the Salamander": *Yes*   "The Sand and the Sieve": *Yes*

What is the climax in *Fahrenheit 451*? *When Montag is standing in front of his burning house, trying to decide how to escape Beatty and the Mechanical Hound.*

What is Montag's major decision? *He burns Beatty and runs.*

What other options might have been open to him? *Answers will vary. Running, as Professor Faber suggests. Turning the hose on the fire engine for an explosion, a diversion, to allow time for his escape, and so on.*

What happens during the resolution phase of *Fahrenheit 451*? *Montag finds the "hobos" and is accepted into the book people's circle. They watch the bombing of the city together and decide to return to it to help its citizens rebuild on a firmer foundation.*

Check the box that best describes which ending Ray Bradbury uses in *Fahrenheit 451*: *Ironic. Montag has lost his wife, his job, his house, his city. He has gained a love and respect for books and the knowledge they contain. He has gained new friends and is not alone.*

Write a summation of the plot of *Fahrenheit 451* using 50 words or fewer, as though for a TV schedule: *Answers will vary. Here is a possibility: Montag, a fireman who burns books for a living, hides and reads forbidden books after he meets an unconventional girl and a professor. When he is discovered as a traitor, he must flee for his life.*

Up or Down?

Teacher, students are learning about endings. An up ending is when the hero goes home happy. Everything turned out well for him. This is fairly unbelievable and rarely used in today's fiction.

A down ending is when the hero does not gain his goal. He meets with failure. This type of ending is popular with some writers but only serves to depress readers or shore up their cynicism.

An ironic ending is when the hero loses something and gains something. This is a believable ending. Most stories end this way. *Fahrenheit 451 has an ironic ending: Montag loses much and gains much.*

Lesson 6

Motifs Again

Animals and Nature
The fire trucks are called two different animals. What are they? *Dragon and Salamander. (37, 108, 114)*

Find one instance in *Fahrenheit 451* in which books are burning and write the nature/animal images below:

- *"A book lit...like a white pigeon...wings fluttering...was like a snowy feather...They fell like slaughtered birds" (34).*
- *"The books lay like great mounds of fishes left to dry" (35).*
- *"Each becomes a black butterfly" (72).*
- *"...the floor littered with swarms of black moths that had died..." (73).*
- *"...their covers torn off and spilled out like swan feathers, the incredible books..."(109).*
- *"The books leapt and danced like roasted birds, their wings ablaze with red and yellow feathers" (110).*

Paradoxes

We've already mentioned the Mechanical Hound, which "slept but did not sleep, lived but did not live" (21). What does Bradbury mean when he describes this monster/machine in this way? Write your answer below or discuss it with someone. *He is referring to the lifelikeness the Hound has, the animal attributes it was given (it has eyes and paws, and nostrils; it has the ability to sniff, to hunt, to react quickly) but also its machine qualities (made of brass, copper, and steel; ruby glass for eyes, sensitive nylon nose hairs, eight legs instead of four). He is also referring to the emotional response the Hound engenders, which creates more fear than any live dog could do.*

Find the paradox on pages 9 and 10. Write the phrases below: *"The room was not empty"/"The room was indeed empty."*

Mirror Images

Find the references to the moon or moonlight on pages 4, 10, 89, 134, and 136.

- *Page 4: "...her face as bright as snow in the moonlight..."*
- *Page 10: "...he did not want the moon to come into the room..."*
- *Page 89: "The moon rose in the sky as Montag walked..."*
- *Page 134: "He saw the moon low in the sky now. The moon there, and the light of the moon caused by what? By the sun, of course."*
- *Page 136: "Then, she would be gone from the warm window and appear again upstairs in her moon-whitened room."*

Allusions to Christian Stories or Phrases

Readers in 1953 would have readily understood the allusions to Bible stories; however, today's readers are not as Bible literate and might miss the references. Who alludes to the "Lord of all Creation" and walking on water? How is he using those references? Write your answer here: *Page 111, Beatty. Derisively, trying to intimidate Montag*

And who, near the end of the story, is the "odd minority crying in the wilderness"? Write your answer here: *Granger, p. 146; they'll have the books in their heads and will be able to "be of some use in the world." They will also be in a position to warn people about the foolishness of bowing to special interest groups in the matter of literature and of the dangers of not taking time to read, think and discuss what they find in books.*

Writers' Device: The Telling Detail

The **telling detail** is the recurring detail that makes the character come alive for the reader. In this case, Clarisse is always connected with something from nature.

Lesson 7

Complete the Online Quizzes and Opinion Survey

Teacher, students are instructed to go to http://WritingWithSharonWatson.com/illuminating-literature-when-worlds-collide-gateway/ to get links to complete the following:
- "Yes, I read it" quiz—graded online for you
- Literary Terms Quiz (ironic ending, motifs, allusions, telling detail, exposition/normalcy, inciting incident, rising action/rising conflict, climax, dénouement/resolution/falling action, utopia, dystopia)—graded online for you
- Opinion Survey—no grade, but answers to the opinion questions may help you develop a strategy for your discussion time.

Password for all online quizzes and the survey for *Fahrenheit 451*: BRADBURY.

Teacher, if you prefer a paper quizzes, you'll find them in *Illuminating Literature: When Worlds Collide, Quiz and Answer Manual,* available for sale at http://writingwithsharonwatson.com/illuminating-literature-when-worlds-collide.

Opinion questions have no correct answer; students are graded on participation. Their answers to the opinion questions may help you develop a strategy for your discussion time.

Student instructions: After you complete the quiz, a report with the questions, your answers, the correct answers, and your score will be sent to the email address you signed in with. Print it off and show it to your teacher.

Teacher, students are allowed two attempts for the "Yes, I read it" quiz and the literary terms quiz but only one attempt for the opinion survey.

Lesson 8

What Is Censorship?

What is censorship? If asked, could you give a definition of it? Join the clash of opinions on this topic!

Below is a list of situations. Read these actual events and circle the numbers of the examples you believe to be censorship:

1. A librarian decides to buy certain books for the library and decides not to buy others based on their content.
2. A mother disciplines her child for saying swear words.
3. A teacher considers her reading list for the upcoming year; some books are included while others don't make the cut because they don't agree with her worldview.
4. A newspaper editor decides what is newsworthy and ignores other news items that come over the wire.
5. Minority or special interest groups demand that certain books such as *The Merchant of Venice, Tom Sawyer,* or the Bible be taken off a school's reading list.
6. A movie executive reading scripts consistently chooses particular kinds while rejecting others based on their content.
7. Concerned citizens write to a broadcast network and boycott its advertisers to protest a certain show.
8. A mother reads a book and decides it is not healthful reading material for her child at that age.
9. The United States disallows the song "Sentimental Journey" to be broadcast on the airwaves during WWII, thinking that it might demoralize the homesick troops.
10. The Ayatollah Khomeini, in an Islamic revolution in Iran in the 1980s, dictates to women what to wear, how to walk, what to read, what not to read, to whom to speak and how, not to laugh out loud, how large their earrings can be, not to wear makeup, and how to appear as invisible as possible so as to not be "seductive."
11. A country makes a "hate speech" law in which citizens are not allowed to speak negatively about or disagree with certain other citizens and their views on politically charged subjects such as homosexuality.
12. A school tells a student not to pray or use the name of Jesus in her graduation speech.
13. The movie industry uses a rating system to keep people under 17 from viewing R-rated movies in theaters.
14. A student decides not to read Harry Potter books because of the witchcraft elements.
15. A government reads its soldiers letters in times of war and crosses out questionable passages in order to make sure that no compromising information leaks to the enemy.
16. The manager of a radio station takes a certain singer off the play list after that singer makes what are considered insensitive or politically incorrect statements.
17. A library puts a filter on its Internet computers so patrons cannot view pornography.
18. A Communist government bans and burns all Bibles and punishes those who have them.
19. An Islamic government refuses to air certain TV shows from the West because of the immoral content.
20. New believers in Christ burn their sorcery scrolls, worth a fortune, in public in Ephesus (Acts 19:17-29).
21. A choir director alters the words to "O Holy Night" and other Christmas carols for a community concert in order to delete references to Jesus and a "dear Savior's birth."
22. Policy makers in government, the media, and public-relations offices decide which words and phrases to quit using, calling them politically incorrect, and substitute other words and phrases (euphemisms) in their place.

Pause now and put a check mark next to the ones you think are the right thing to do. Which of the above list did you choose as examples of censorship? Take some time out to discuss this with someone and to discuss what censorship is. *Answers will vary.*

A Dark and Sinister Warning

As promised at the beginning of this chapter, there is a darker and more sinister warning encrypted into the narrative of *Fahrenheit 451*. And by now you have probably discovered it. Write what you think it is in the space below: *Answers will vary. Something like this will be appropriate: If we allow ourselves to become distracted by our technology and do not allow ourselves time to think and to act upon what we have thought about, if we chose technology over the very natural things in life, then we will lose everything—our technology, our books, the important information, the natural world around us, our ability to think and act, and even our freedom.*

In Ray Bradbury's own words on *Fahrenheit 451*: "I was worried about people being turned into morons by TV." [14]

Lesson 9

Questions for Discussion

Teacher, before delving into the discussion questions, ask students these questions:

1.   What questions do you have about *Fahrenheit 451*?
2.   What aspects of this book appealed to you?
3.   What is your impression of this book?

These preliminary questions will help to clear up any misunderstandings or miscomprehensions from the books, and they'll get students talking during the discussion session because they are open-ended questions. Students can answer other students' questions, too. This pre-discussion time may also serve to answer some of the questions printed below or can be a springboard to any of the aspects of the book you want to focus on.

1. If we are what we memorize, what would *you* be? *Answers will vary.*
2. We humans experience many fears in our lives. One is the fear of missing out or FOMO. Although the name is new, the condition has been around for ages and has only been made worse by our dependence on and addiction to our technology. We're afraid of missing out on whatever else might be going on, brought to us by texts, tweets, posts, and other avenues that make our mobiles or tablets impossible to put down or turn off. Watch this YouTube video https://www.youtube.com/watch?v=KqgaJx5X18Q. How long do you think you could go without looking at your mobile device or tablet? How do

156

you feel when it is unavailable to you? How does our technology connect us? How does it keep us from forming healthy relationships? Would you rather be on your device for thirty minutes or have a face-to-face conversation with someone of your choice? *Answers will vary.*

3. Bradbury includes plenty of reasons why the censorship came about. Name two. *The books don't agree with each other (35), the world is too populous for different opinions (51), people got too busy to think (52-3), minorities and special interest groups spawned controversies(54), people became politically correct (55), nobody wanted controversies (55), didn't begin with the government but with "technology, mass exploitation, and minority pressure" (55), valued peace of mind and happiness over thinking (55-6), "conflicting theory and thought"(59), "we let them go" (78), "The public stopped reading of its own accord" (87), no one wanted or missed the newspapers (85).*

4. Faber's and Granger's opinions are Bradbury's, too. He even puts some of his opinions in Beatty's mouth. What is Bradbury's opinion of public schools? Of reading condensed books? Of TV? *School doesn't improve one's socialization, it doesn't cover a topic thoroughly and with depth, it tells you "what" but it doesn't tell you "why," it doesn't give you time to think through anything, it runs students ragged (27), children are going to school way too young (6), condensed books are "books leveled down to a sort of pastepudding norm" (51), classics are ruined by condensing them (52); Bradbury's views on TV are shown in how harmful the full-wall televisor is to Mildred and to society, who calls the actors their "family" and who are blasted with sound and information without being given an opportunity to think.*

5. In a novel in which books have preeminence by virtue of their illegality, Professor Faber says this surprising thing: "It's not books you need." What does he mean by this? *It is not the books that are special but the information and ideas they contained that are special (78-9). Additionally, important knowledge and wisdom about life can be found in other sources.*

6. According to Professor Faber, what three things are missing? *1) Books of quality that are truthful in their detail and in their ability to touch life, 2) time to think, to enjoy life, to appreciate art, and 3) "the right to carry out actions based on what we learn from the interaction of the first two." (79-80)*

7. According to Mildred and her friends, what should a political candidate's qualifications be? *Handsome, tall, well kempt, a good and clear speaker, not fat, well dressed, a handsome-sounding name, mannerly (93).*

8. What does Bradbury use as justification for Montag murdering Beatty? *Montag had to escape somehow; he later realizes that "Beatty wanted to die" (116); "You did what you had to do. It was coming on for a long time" (125); in addition, **Bradbury narrows down the choice** for Montag: kill or be killed.*

9. What do you think happened to Clarisse, her family, and Professor Faber? *It was reported that Clarisse was hit by a car and her family dragged off, but the reader is left to doubt this information in the light of the media circus that follows Montag and kills a Montag stand-in. Perhaps Professor Faber died in*

the bombing or escaped and will eventually join the book men. His fate is uncertain.

10. An African proverb says, "When an old man dies, a library burns down." What do you think this means? *Answers will vary.*

11. Compare and contrast (think of similarities and differences) among these three events and draw some insightful conclusions: *Answers will vary. Although they are all in self-defense, there are some significant differences. For instance, Miss Pross is defending herself but on behalf of the escaping Lucie. The lead in* The War of the Worlds *supposedly whacked the curate in self-defense, but he never liked the fellow anyway; suspicious motives. Montag was protecting Professor Faber and himself but could have chosen another avenue of escape.*

- The lead whacking the curate in *The War of the Worlds*
- Miss Pross killing Madame Defarge in *A Tale of Two Cities*
- Montag killing Captain Beatty in *Fahrenheit 451*

If You Liked This Book

Teachers, students are viewing and adding to a list of books with similar themes or in similar genres.

This is the end of lesson 9.

Your Choice of Activities

Teacher, please tell students when this is due.

Be the Author—Write a short story.
Be the Author Again—Imitate a passage.
Your Opinion—Tell your opinion in a short essay.
Your Opinion Again—Read quotations and defend your view.
An Ad Campaign—Develop an ad campaign.
Silence Is Golden—Experience silence ("leisure") for a time.
History Buff—Find examples of book burning in history.
You Heard it Here First, Folks—Write a radio version of a scene in *Fahrenheit 451*.
The Artist in You—Create the Mechanical Hound, a room with the "families" in it, or the symbol for the firemen in any medium you choose.

Be the Author
Is there something in *Fahrenheit 451* or in Bradbury's style that has ignited your imagination? Or is there something in your life (like Bradbury's late-night walk that was interrupted by a policeman) upon which you could spin a story? If so, write a short story of your choosing and share it with someone.

Be the Author Again

Near the end of *Fahrenheit 451*, Montag is floating down the river when his foot hits land. This makes him think of a time when he visited a farm, and this leads him to a deep longing. You can read this passage on pages 135-6. Begin with "During the night . . . ," and end with "He stepped from the river."

This moving passage uses the verb "would." This is the conditional tense, a tense filled with a deep desire for something to occur.

Write your own passage of a few paragraphs in which a character longs for something to happen. Use a character you invent or one you already know from another story. Use the "would" of the conditional tense.

Your Opinion

Below are two quotations. Choose one and answer it based on your own knowledge and opinion.

- "There must be something in books, things we can't imagine, to make a woman stay in a burning house; there must be something there." (Montag, p. 48) What is there about books that someone would defend them with her life?
- "Where they have burned books, they will end in burning human beings" (Heinrich Heine). Do you think this is true? If so, cite examples. If not, defend your view.

An Ad Campaign

Mildred asks this question (p. 69): "Why should I read? What *for*?" Write an ad campaign to give people a reason to read and to encourage them to do it. Your ads can be for radio, TV, billboards, or Internet use.

Your Opinion Again

James Barrie stated this: "Nothing that happens after we are twelve matters very much."

Bradbury, on the other hand, said this: "The great thing about my life is that everything I've done is a result of what I was when I was 12 or 13."

Which man do you agree with? Explain your answer in a short essay of about 300-400 words.

Silence Is Golden

Faber's second point in his lesson for Montag is this: leisure. But he doesn't mean time off. He means what we might call today "downtime." He goes on to explain (p. 80):

> "Off-hours, yes. But time to think? If you're not driving a hundred miles an hour, at a clip where you can't think of anything else but the danger, then you're playing some game or sitting in some room where you can't argue with the four-wall televisor. Why? The televisor is 'real.' It is immediate, it has dimension. It tells you what to think and blasts it in. It *must* be right. It *seems* so right. It rushes you on so quickly to its own conclusions, your mind hasn't time to protest, 'What nonsense!'"

For this activity, you will turn off all radios, televisions, VCRs, DVDs, iPods, Internet, mobile devices, and any other form of media, including social media. As much as is possible, let the silence sink in. Give yourself time to *think*. When you jump in the car, don't reach for the radio or your iPod. When you are in your bedroom, don't turn on the radio, TV, Internet, or anything else that speaks or sings or thinks for you. Use your mobile device in emergencies only. Let a parent know what you are doing.

Choose a time period for your experiment—sometime between 24 hours and one week. Record your reactions and thoughts in a journal, or report your results to a friend.

History Buff

Historically, the Bible has been the most banned and burned book ever. But there are plenty of other books that have made it to a banned list. In addition, there have been plenty of 451-degree bonfires around the world through the ages. Research stories of book banning and book burning. Then write a short speech or essay, or make a list of the books or the occasions.

You Heard it Here First, Folks

As you might remember, *The War of the Worlds* was written in radio announcer format and broadcast in the United States in the 1930s, causing much panic and fear. Now it's your turn. Write a scene or two from *Fahrenheit 451* in the style of a radio news announcer, as though the event is happening at that moment. Choose your scene for its impact or its action and capitalize on it.

The Artist in You

Our imaginations can give us mental pictures when we read an author's work. Interpret the author's words and make them tangible. Choose any medium you prefer and create the Mechanical Hound, the room with the "families," the symbol the firemen use as their insignia, or any other part of *Fahrenheit 451*. Or create a new cover for the book.

Teacher, on the next page, you'll find the Grading Grid for *Fahrenheit 451*. The grid is marked for a possible 100 points per book. Please feel free to adjust it to your needs and expectations. You have permission to copy it as many times as needed for your own class, co-op, reading group, book-of-the-month club, or family.

Grading Grid for *Fahrenheit 451*

Student's Name: _____

Online "Yes, I read it" quiz, graded online. 1-10 points	
Online literary terms quiz, graded online. 1-10 points	
Participation in opinion questions online. 1-10 points	
Quality of participation in discussions. 1-20 points	
Successful completion of lessons and assignments. 1-20 points	
Successful completion of activity. 1-10 points	
Finished reading the book. 1-20 points.	
Total grade for *Fahrenheit 451*	

Writing with
Sharon Watson

Chapter 8: *The Screwtape Letters*

HarperCollins   ISBN: 978-0-06-065293-7

Facebook Posts

If your group or co-op meets monthly, you may want to keep in touch with the students and keep them interested in the novels by creating a secret Facebook group for only them and their parents. Feel free to devise your own questions or find your own links to interesting material.

- To get us in the mood for reading a book penned by a demon, check out this video of strange sounds that have been recorded worldwide: https://www.youtube.com/watch?v=hvhuXgZ_LQs&sns=em. Assuming this is real and not a hoax, what do you think the source of these strange sounds is?

- "No. Space was the wrong name. Older thinkers had been wiser when they named it simply the heavens" (C. S. Lewis in *Out of the Silent Planet*). In the best tradition of Anne Shirley from *Anne of Green Gables*, who gave the name "the Lake of Shining Waters" to a pond, rename something in your life. Tell us the old and new names.

- You get to hear C. S. Lewis in his own voice in this video! It's one of the surviving talks from the BBC during WWII that he eventually wrote into *Mere Christianity*. https://www.youtube.com/watch?v=JHxs3gdtV8A. What are your impressions?

- C. S. Lewis, J. R. R. Tolkien, and other writers formed a club called the Inklings. Nice double meaning, don't you think? Anyway, they met every Tuesday morning to talk, read each other's manuscripts, and be philosophical and practical about the world and writing. I think Guy Montag would have liked to attend the club!

  You can read more about it here: http://www.scriptoriumnovum.com/l/inklings01.html. If you were to attend a meeting once a week, what would it be? What would you do?

- For a fun doodle on C. S. Lewis's words on science and religion, go to https://www.youtube.com/watch?v=AJu0oYvi-cY. What did you learn that you didn't know before?

- In letter 8 of *The Screwtape Letters*, we read this from Screwtape: "Our cause is never more in danger than when a human . . . looks round upon a universe from which every trace of Him [God] seems to have vanished, and asks why he has been forsaken, and still obeys." Tell about a time when things looked dire for you but you still obeyed and believed in God.

- Screwtape writes that the patient will appear "intolerant" and "Puritanical" if he stops hanging out with and laughing at the jokes of a group of unspiritual, cynical people. This ties in with something Peter wrote in I Peter 4:4 that people doing awful or wicked things will think it's strange that you don't join them, and when you don't, they "heap abuse" on you (ridicule or call you names, like "intolerant"). Tell of a time when doing the right thing could be perceived as intolerant or Puritanical.

- For another amazing doodle on *The Screwtape Letters* read by Andy Serkis (Gollum in *The Lord of the Rings* movies) go to https://www.youtube.com/watch?v=D3MWVMKKY3A . The Eagle and the Child, which you see in the first frame, is the pub where C. S. Lewis, J. R. R. Tolkien, and others met weekly for the Inklings. What are your reactions to this doodle?

- Is "good only what man is conditioned to approve"? Okay, all you thinkers out there, check out this super-cool doodle video on C. S. Lewis's explanation of "The Poison of Subjectivity" and how it affects our thinking today. https://www.youtube.com/watch?v=Lgcd6jvsCFs

- What question would you like to ask C. S. Lewis?

Before You Read the Book

Lesson 1

Suggested Reading and Homework Plan: Preview

Week 1:
- ❑ Complete lessons 1-3.
- ❑ Complete lesson 4: Read letters 1-6 in *The Screwtape Letters*. Answer any questions from these letters in your Novel Notebook assigned by your teacher.

Week 2: Lesson 5
- ❑ Read letters 7-19 in *The Screwtape Letters*. Answer any questions from these letters in your Novel Notebook assigned by your teacher.

Week 3: Lesson 6
- ❑ Read letters 20-31 in *The Screwtape Letters* . If your version of the book has any back matter (stuff after letter 31, like "Screwtape Proposes a Toast"), read it. Answer any questions from these letters in your Novel Notebook assigned by your teacher.

Week 4:
- ❑ Choose your activity (see the end of the chapter) and begin work on it.
- ❑ Complete lessons 7-9.
- ❑ Complete your activity. Your teacher will tell you when this is due.

Imitate!

If your pastor or priest gave a sermon or homily titled "How to Succumb to a Temptation," I imagine that about half the congregation would understand that the subject was being treated in a satirical manner. That is, the speaker is using satire to fix a problem. The point of the talk would be show how we can fall prey to temptation, thus giving listeners tools with which they could avoid succumbing to it.

And, I'm guessing, the other half of the congregation would be so offended and incensed that they would march out.

What happened? Well, satire is meant to be understood figuratively, not in a literal sense. The angry half of the congregation did not understand the tone of the message. They took it literally, just as some readers did when Jonathan Swift suggested in *A Modest Proposal* that the overpopulation of Ireland could be fixed by selling their babies to rich English gentry as food. He even provided recipes.

Here are two items in the news today as I write this: terrorism and the Ebola virus. Since we can't seem to stop terrorism any other way, I suggest we infect all terrorists with the Ebola virus. Stop them dead in their tracks.

No, of course, I don't mean it. I'm being satirical—proposing an outlandish fix to a thorny problem. Writers use satire to wake up people and make them think about workable solutions to problems.

Now it's your turn to write a satirical letter or advice column. Think of a problem you would like to fix and then treat it in an outlandish way, as Swift does in *A Modest Proposal*.

Teacher: If you have time in class, you may want to use this as an in-class writing opportunity so students can learn by what their peers have written. If you are teaching a co-op, the paragraph can be due in a week or emailed to you.

Lesson 2

Meet C. S. Lewis

Students are reading about Lewis's life. Write two things below that interested you about C. S. Lewis: *Answers will vary.*

Lesson 3

Literary License

Students are learning that Lewis created "families" of demons, even though demons and angels don't have families (Matt. 22:30). He was not creating a new doctrine. This is called **literary license**.

Literary Terms: Epistolary Novel and Satire

Epistolary novel: one written in the form of letters.

Satire: writing to fix a problem in an outlandish fashion. Students are given examples of satire.

Writers' Device: Connotation

Denotation: the dictionary definition
Connotation: how people react to the word, the feelings it conjures up, as in the creepy words "Screwtape" and "Wormwood."

The Front Matter and a Heads Up

Students are learning what the front matter is (everything before the first page of the book or novel, like the copyright info, dedication page, and introduction).

Read the dedication page and the preface, and then STOP to answer these questions:
1. What are the "two equal and opposite errors" people can make about devils? *"To disbelieve in their existence" (the materialist); to believe but "feel an excessive and unhealthy interest" in demons.*
2. What must readers remember as they read this collection of letters? *The devil is a liar.*
3. To whom is this book dedicated? *J. R. R. Tolkien*

In *The Screwtape Letters*, Satan is referred to as "Our Father Below," and God is "the Enemy." Be aware of this flip-flop when you read.

This is the end of Lesson 3.

Suggested Reading and Homework Plan

Week 1:
- ❑ Complete lessons 1-3.
- ❑ Complete lesson 4: Read letters 1-6 in *The Screwtape Letters*. Answer any questions from these letters in your Novel Notebook assigned by your teacher. If you have not finished your Week One tasks yet, complete them now.

Week 2: Lesson 5
- ❑ Read letters 7-19 in *The Screwtape Letters*. Answer any questions from these letters in your Novel Notebook assigned by your teacher.

Week 3: Lesson 6
- ❑ Read letters 20-31 in *The Screwtape Letters*. If your version of the book has any back matter (stuff after letter 31, like "Screwtape Proposes a Toast"), read it. Answer any questions from these letters in your Novel Notebook assigned by your teacher.

Week 4:
- ❑ Choose your activity (see the end of the chapter) and begin work on it.
- ❑ Complete lessons 7-9.
- ❑ Complete your activity. **Your teacher will tell you when this is due.**

Lesson 4

Letters 1-6

Please select three of the letters in this section to answer in your Novel Notebook.

Or ask your teacher which letters or which questions below you should focus on and then answer the questions he or she assigns.

To download a free Novel Notebook with the questions already in it, go to http://writingwithsharonwatson.com/illuminating-literature-when-worlds-collide-gateway/ .

Letter 1
1. Who are Screwtape and Wormwood? *Uncle and nephew, both devils*
2. Write below any example of this shift from the arena of right and wrong to the arena of other values or catchwords. You may use examples from life or from literature. *Answers may vary.*
3. List the tactics/temptations below: *Answers may vary.*
    - *Move him from "true" and "false" evaluations of ideas. Let him use other labels: courageous, practical, outworn, and so forth.*
    - *"Fuddle" him.*
    - *Make him focus on the stream of sense experiences, not on arguments, reason, and logic.*

Letter 2
1. What do you think is the purpose of his patient coming to Christ so early in the book? *Answers will vary. Maybe Lewis wanted to speak to Christians and the particular temptations they are up against.*
2. Why, according to Screwtape, is it harder to tempt someone who successfully has come through this initial phase of disillusionment and dryness? *"They become much less dependent on emotion..."(8).*
3. List the tactics/temptations below: *Answers may vary.*
    - *Focus him on the people and other irksome things about his particular church, not the Church historic and triumphant.*

Letter 3
List the tactics/temptations below: *Answers may vary.*
- *"Build up...a good settled habit of mutual annoyance; daily pinpricks." Allow his mother's little idiosyncrasies to bother him, but he'll think he's perfect.*
- *Don't let him think his conversion has anything to do with an outward duty, only an inward life.*
- *Keep his prayers "spiritual," not practical. This will keep him focused on her sins, i.e., what irritates him, not on her real needs.*
- *Constantly remind him of what irks him about her and lead him to think she does it on purpose, to annoy him. Do not let him suspect that he can be annoying.*

- *Make him over-sensitive to his mother's voice intonations and words while giving himself full permission to say anything in any way.*

Letter 4

1. Screwtape describes what people "see" when they pray to God. What images of God come into your mind when you are praying? *Answers will vary.*
2. List the tactics/temptations below: *Answers may vary.*
   - *Keep him from any serious praying, but cultivate in him a "vaguely devotional mood" or a "desired feeling." Try to produce a feeling, not a prayer.*
   - *Keep him praying to an object or place or his own imagination of God, not to God himself, the "invisible Presence."*

Letter 5

1. What is the real business of devils? *"Undermining faith and preventing the formation of virtues" (22).*
2. Write what it is like in the demons' world (pp. 21-2): *"The reward of all our labours—the anguish and bewilderment of a human soul" (21). "A brim-full living chalice of despair and horror and astonishment which you can raise to your lips as often as you please" (22) and "incessant hunger(22). This is the first intimation of devils feeding off their victims.*
3. What is the lie you find on page 23? *"He [God] is so unfair."*
4. List the tactics/temptations: *Answers may vary.*
   - *Show him a terror-filled future.*
   - *"Catch your man when his reason is temporarily suspended."*

Letter 6

List the tactics/temptations below: *Answers may vary.*
- *Don't let him deal with the fear but keep him focused on the things he is afraid of, as though those are what he is to bear with patience.*
- *Let him display toward his neighbor or mother his malice for German leaders; let him save his benevolent feelings for people he does not know.*

Lesson 5

Letters 7-19

Please select three of the letters in this section to answer in your Novel Notebook.

Or ask your teacher which letters or which questions below you should focus on and then answer the questions he or she assigns.

Pace yourself. This is a week-long lesson.

Letter 7

List the tactics/temptations below: *Answers may vary.*

- *If he begins to suspect that you exist, make him think of "something in red tights." Because he doesn't believe in this, he will not believe in you.*
- *Encourage all extremes except extreme devotion to the Enemy.*
- *Keep the Church small so people will acquire the pride of a clique.*
- *Let him add either patriotism or pacifism to his religion. Then, let his religion be merely an addendum to the cause.*

Letter 8

1. Explain in your own words the Law of Undulation. *Answers will vary. People go through periods of great highs and lows, richness and dryness. It is natural because they are of the earth but have spirits.*

2. How do the devils consider humans? (Think of what the Martians in *The War of the Worlds* wanted to do to the humans.) *"To us a human is primarily food" (38) and "We want cattle who can finally become food" (39).*

3. What puts the devils' cause at most risk? *"Our cause is never more in danger than when a human…looks round upon a universe from which every trace of Him seems to have vanished, and asks why he has been forsaken, and still obeys" (40).*

4. List the tactics/temptations below: *Answers may vary.*
   - *Make good use of the trough (low) times.*
   - *Interfere with their will when they are down.*

Letter 9

List the tactics/temptations below: *Answers may vary.*

- *Exploit the dry periods; tempt him with sex or other sensual pleasures like too much drink—any pleasure not in its "healthy and normal and satisfying form."*
- *Keep the Law of Undulation out of his mind. Make him try to recover "his old feelings by sheer will-power" or make him think that this is all there is or that this is as good as it gets, that his first zeal was "adolescent" or a phase or excessive.*
- *Tell him the trough is permanent. Convince him that his religious phase is dying away.*

Letter 10

List the tactics/temptations below: *Answers may vary.*

- *Encourage him to play up to his new, cynical friends and not acknowledge his Christianity. Feed his desire to be accepted by those whose qualities he values.*
- *Encourage him to live two parallel lives: one with his cynical, shallow friends, and one as a Christian—to be something he is not.*
- *Persuade him to think that teachings on morals, friends, virtues, time, and the act of not going out with those people are all "Puritanical," a word with a useful negative connotation.*

Letter 11

1. What piece of information do you learn about demons on page 53? *They don't know what the cause of joy and joyful laughter is.*
2. What are the four categories of human laughter? *Joy, fun, the joke proper, and flippancy.*
3. What does Proverbs 26:18-19 say about doing something questionable and then calling it a joke? *It's like a madman shooting deadly arrows.*
4. "Nothing shows a man's character more than what he laughs at" (Johann Wolfgang Von Goethe). What do you laugh at? *Answers will vary.*
5. List the tactics/temptations below: *Answers may vary.*
    - *Teach him that he can get away with almost anything if he does it in fun or calls it a joke.*
    - *Show him how to treat his sins or shortcomings as jokes.*

Letter 12

List the tactics/temptations below: *Answers may vary.*
- *Keep him thinking that all the habits and decisions he's made that have led him farther away from God are "trivial and revocable."*
- *Keep any feelings vague he may feel about not doing very well. This keeps him from repenting.*
- *Keep him in a number of small sins that separate him from the Enemy.*

Letter 13

1. Do you ever see the "patient" directly, or is it always through the demons' eyes? What is the patient's name? *Through the demons' eyes; we never know his name.*
2. What brought the patient out of his spiritual nosedive? *He read a good book because he enjoyed it, and he took a walk and tea at a place he really liked, not somewhere his new friends like. In other words, he experienced a simple pleasure and woke up from his tedium.*
3. Disregard the intimation that a Christian can fall away after he's saved. Some Christians believe this; others don't. Lewis is using that possibility to heighten the conflict and the tension.
4. List the tactics/temptations below: *Answers may vary.*
    - *Keep him believing that "vanity, bustle, irony, and expensive tedium" are pleasures.*
    - *"Substitute the standards of the World, or convention, or fashion for a human's own real likings and dislikings." (Like what everyone else is liking.)*
    - *Keep him from converting his repentance into actions.*

Letter 14

List the tactics/temptations below: *Answers will vary.*
- *Make him aware of his virtues. This will create pride.*
- *Pervert true humility by giving him a low or high estimation of his abilities.*

- *Fix his mind on an opinion of his talents—whether low or high. Then he will be focused on himself, not on the Enemy.*

Letter 15
List the tactics/temptations below: *Answers will vary.*
- *Tempt him with either tortured fear or stupid confidence.*
- *Tempt him to live in the Past or the Future, but never in the Present, for "the Present is the point at which time touches eternity....We want a man hag-ridden by the Future."*

Letter 16
List the tactics/temptations below: *Answers may vary.*
- *Attach him to a faction in a church that is unrelated to any doctrine. On doctrine, keep him lukewarm.*

Letter 17
List the tactics/temptations below: *Answers may vary.*
- *Get him to be really irked at having to deny himself something he really wants. Then charity, justice, and obedience go out the door.*
- *Make him believe that excessive physical exercise aids chastity.*

Letter 18
1. What is "our Father's first great victory," according to Screwtape (p. 93)? The fall of man. *The fall of man.*
2. What is the insight you find into the demons' world on page 94? *They are all in competition with each other, sucking will and freedom out of a weaker one and into a stronger one.*
3. List the tactics/temptations below: *Answers may vary.*
   - *Persuade humans to rely on a feeling of being in love as a basis for continuing a marriage and that, if there is no feeling, they can divorce.*
   - *Persuade them that marrying because they're "in love" is the best, the only, way and that any other motive is low and cynical.*

Letter 19
1. What is the lie you find on pages 99 to 100? *It is impossible for God to love humans.*
2. What two things do you learn about Satan ("Our Father Below") in this chapter? *His fall—or his version of his fall—and the fact that he can't understand love.*
3. List the tactics/temptations below: *Answers may vary.*
   - *Move him into a marriage that will make his Christianity difficult for him.*

Lesson 6

Letters 20-31

Please select three of the letters in this section to answer in your Novel Notebook.

Or ask your teacher which letters or which questions below you should focus on and then answer the questions he or she assigns.

Pace yourself. This is a week-long lesson.

Letter 20
List the tactics/temptations below: *Answers may vary.*
- *Persuade him to get rid of a temptation by giving into it.*
- *Tie him to a wife who will lead him away from the Enemy.*
- *Produce a sexual "taste," a fashion in every age that dictates what beauty or desirability is in clothing, bodies, facial features, and so forth. Then encourage him to reject anyone who doesn't fit that mold.*
- *Immodest dressing is "frank" and "healthy" and "getting back to nature."*

Letter 21
1. What is Lewis' analogy for the body ownership thing? *A young prince still under the rule of his advisors comes to believe that he owns everything.*
2. List the tactics/temptations below: *Answers may vary.*
    - *Make him feel injured by someone, and therefore, ill-tempered.*
    - *Make him think his time is his own.*
    - *Encourage a sense of ownership. "Much of the modern resistance to chastity comes from men's belief that they 'own' their bodies...in which they find themselves without their consent."*

Letter 22
1. What lie about God do you read on page 118? *God is vulgar and has a bourgeois mind.*
2. What do you learn about the demons' world on page 117? *They must pay for each blunder.*
3. What does Screwtape mean by "to unite you to myself in an indissoluble embrace" (p. 121)? *To consume or eat him.*
4. Read 2 Corinthians 2:14-16. What does Paul say about aromas and smells? *The knowledge of God is fragrant; we are "the aroma of Christ"; saved people perceive this odor as a life-giving fragrance, but lost people consider it "the smell of death."* What is the "deadly odour," the "impenetrable mystery," and the "vast obscenity" Screwtape writes about (119)? *The presence of God.*
5. Make lists of the similarities and the differences between "Music and Silence" and "Noise." *Answers will vary.*

Letter 23
List the tactics/temptations below: *Answers may vary.*

- *Corrupt his spirituality by 1) creating a "historical Jesus" by "suppression at one point and exaggeration at another," 2) distracting his mind from who Jesus really is and what He did, encouraging a theory of what he supposedly championed, 3) destroying his devotional life, substituting a "remote, shadowy" figure for the "real presence" of God, and 4) getting rid of the conviction of sin.*
- *Keep his Christianity separate from his political life, avoiding any just society.*
- *Use Christianity as a means to an end, say, social justice. "Believe this, not because it is true, but for some other reason."*

Letter 24
List the tactics/temptations below: *Answers may vary.*

- *Get him to imitate his girlfriend's defect—spiritual pride. He will think he is smarter than he really is. Then he will differentiate himself from nonbelievers and think himself better than they.*
- *Confuse him.*

Letter 25

1. What is Lewis' example of a perfect blend of change and permanence? *The seasons change each year, but each season is the same in its own time period.*
2. What kind of generation does Screwtape warn against enthusiasm? *The worldly and lukewarm.*
3. What kind of generation does Screwtape warn against Puritanism? *Lecherous.*
4. List the tactics/temptations below: *Answers may vary.*
   - *Pervert Christianity by blending it with some other cause or idea.*
   - *Exploit the human disdain for the "Same Old Thing." This will produce heresies. Twist the natural desire for change into a demand for absolute novelty.*
   - *For "unchanged," read "stagnant."*
   - *Use Fashions (not clothing) to distract men from their real need and dangers.*

Letter 26
List the tactics/temptations below: *Answers may vary.*

- *Make them believe that however kind they are to each other now, they should (or will) be throughout their relationship. This can end in arguments and disillusionment.*
- *Mutual falseness and not noticing someone else's Unselfishness = Bitterness.*

Letter 27
List the tactics/temptations below: *Answers may vary.*

- *Turn him against praying for his daily needs and the things that weigh on his mind. Undermine his idea of the need for prayer by making him suspect that it is "absurd" and will have no results.*
- *Never ask whether a statement is true.*
- *"Cut every generation off from all others."*

Letter 28

List the tactics/temptations below: *Answers may vary.*
- *Convince him that the "earth can be turned into Heaven at some future date by politics or eugenics or 'science' or psychology."*

Letter 29

1. What do you learn about demons on page 159? *They cannot produce any virtue.*
2. List the tactics/temptations below: *Answers may vary.*
   - *Aim for either cowardice or bravery with pride.*
   - *Stir up hatred, if not on his behalf, at least on the behalf of the women and children.*
   - *Combine hatred with fear.*
   - *Aggravate shame in order to produce Despair.*

Letter 30

1. What do you learn about the demons' world on page 165? *If they do not produce victims, they become victims themselves.*
2. Explain what Screwtape means by "real" life. *The world is what you can see; Christianity is a fantasy. "Real" means the bare physical facts or the emotional effect those facts have on human consciousness. Or, if something can make you despair, those "spiritual elements are the main reality and to ignore them is to be an escapist." "His emotion at the sight of human entrails...is Reality and his emotion at the sight of happy children...is mere sentiment [not real]." All the bad things in life are "real," but the happy things are sentimental slop.*
3. What is your definition of "real" life? *Answers will vary.*
4. List the tactics/temptations below:
   - *Encourage him to keep a subjective haze around nice things, and a "reality" around nasty things.*

Letter 31

1. What do you learn about the demons' world on page 171? *Screwtape considers Wormwood food, a tasty morsel.*
2. What interesting fact do you learn about demons on page 175? *Demons do not know what God is up to! Yay!*
3. What happens to the patient? *He dies in a bombing raid in London.*
4. When the patient sees reality at the point of his death, what does he see and understand? *He sees Wormwood and understands what part the demon has played in his life. He sees angels ("Them") and understands what they have done for him. He sees God ("Him") and feels the pain of his sins and the worship*

of falling before Jesus (who "wears the form of a Man") in light and clarity. He understands that his doubts about God "became . . . ridiculous" (172).

5. How does Screwtape describe Hell? *The Kingdom of Noise.*
6. How does Screwtape describe God? *He is a "blinding, suffocating fire."*
7. Look up these pages and write down what Screwtape calls humans: 65, 72, 79, 94, 131, 153, 157, and 173. This is reminiscent of H. G. Wells' description of humans in *The War of the Worlds. Little vermin, hairless bipeds, the creature, the organism, young barbarian, the creature, animals, this thing of earth and slime.*

Screwtape Proposes a Toast

1. Upon what have the demons been feasting? *The anguish of human souls.*
2. Cerberus (193)—in Greek mythology, the many-headed dog that guarded the entrance to Hades.
3. Bell-wether (194)—the lead sheep that has a bell around its neck; therefore, someone in a leadership role whom people will follow.
4. Give an example of complaints about people who don't fit the current mold or who are considered "uppity" because they don't join in. You may use examples you've heard, read, or thought. *Answers will vary.*
5. What warnings does Lewis put in this section that are relevant for today's culture? *Answers will vary.*

After You've Read the Book

Lesson 7

Five-Star Report

Students are filling out a graph to show how they felt about *The Screwtape Letters.* 1 = Couldn't stand it. 5 = Loved it!

Teacher, the reward for reading the book can be devil's food cake or cupcakes.

Colliding Worlds

What worlds are colliding with each other? What people, philosophies, cultures, and so forth, are in conflict with each other? Fill in the list below. The first one is done for you:

1. Demons versus humans
2. *Physical, seen world versus spiritual, unseen world*
3. *Satan versus God*
4. *Hell versus Heaven*
5. *Evil versus Good*
6. *Right thinking versus "fuddled" thinking*

In the area of conflict, who seems to have the most struggles in this book—the patient, Wormwood, or Screwtape? Put your answer here: *Answers will vary.*

It is interesting that in *Screwtape*, these conflicts are supposed to highlight our own conflicts with the devil and his tactics. Was C. S. Lewis successful in this? *Answers will vary.*

Answer the following questions about conflict in *Screwtape*:

1. How does Lewis keep you from siding with or identifying with Screwtape or his bumbling nephew? How does he lead you to have empathy for the patient? *Answers will vary. Lewis keeps the demons' world rife with hatred, competition, punishments, and a sense that in the end, they will lose. He chose to highlight temptations that all of us are familiar with and battle often. They obviously hate us and want to destroy us here and in eternity.*
2. What temptations or tactics does C. S. Lewis leave out? *Answers will vary.*
3. If the patient had been a woman, what different temptations or tactics might have been included? (For more insights into temptations particular to women, read John Milton's amazing *Paradise Lost*, Book IX, beginning with the line "His fraudulent temptation thus began.") *Answers will vary. Perhaps flattery, tempting her away from her husband because her beauty is too important to be confined to one man, encourage her to have "experiences," i.e., hook up with many men, convince her that being a stay-at-home mother is for lazy women, and so forth.*
4. What tactics/temptations from *The Screwtape Letters* mean something to you because they have caused conflict in your life? *Answers will vary.*
5. How does the patient die? What do you think of this way that Lewis chooses to end the conflict? *Killed in a bombing raid. Answers will vary.*

Lesson 8

Complete the Online Quizzes and Survey

Teacher, students are instructed to go to http://WritingWithSharonWatson.com/illuminating-literature-when-worlds-collide-gateway/ to get links to complete the following:

- "Yes, I read it" quiz—graded online for you
- Literary Terms Quiz (epistolary, connotation, denotation, satire, empathetic character, euphemism, literary element, theme)—graded online for you.
- Opinion Survey—no grade, but answers to the opinion questions may help you develop a strategy for your discussion time.

Password for all online quizzes and the survey for *The Screwtape Letters*: LEWIS.

Teacher, if you prefer printed quizzes, you'll find them in *Illuminating Literature: When Worlds Collide, Quiz and Answer Manual,* available for sale at http://writingwithsharonwatson.com/illuminating-literature-when-worlds-collide.

Opinion questions have no correct answer; students are graded on participation. Their answers to the opinion questions may help you develop a strategy for your discussion time.

Student instructions: After you complete the quiz, a report with the questions, your answers, the correct answers, and your score will be sent to the email address you signed in with. Print it off and show it to your teacher.

Teacher, students are allowed two attempts for the "Yes, I read it" quiz and the literary terms quiz but only one attempt for the opinion survey.

Vocabulary Quizzola for *The Screwtape Letters*

Objectives:
- To reinforce good vocabulary habits and awareness.
- To gain a grade, which is separate from the Grading Grid.

Directions: Match the definition on the right with the correct word on the left by entering the letter in the correct blank. The numbers to the right of the words indicate the page numbers where each word can be found in the HarperCollins version for this course of *The Screwtape Letters*. **Ask your teacher if this is an open-book quiz.**

_P_1. Aberrations, 4
_G_2. Anodyne, 44
_X_3. Antithesis, 47
_O_4. Eradicate, 66
_B_5. Bipeds, 72
_U_6. Insipid, 83
_Z_7. Chastity, 90
_Q_8. Panacea, 94
_D_9. Copulation, 95
_R_10. Mooted, 100
_M_11. Meritorious, 102
_N_12. Bourgeois, 118
_F_13. Heresies, 135
_T_14. Avarice, 137
_J_15. Rapacious, 137
_A_16. Lasciviousness, 137
_C_17. Endemic, 138
_K_18. Feckless, 138
_L_19. Lecherous, 138
_E_20. Philological, 141
_W_21. Altruisms, 144
_I_22. Inculcating, 150
_S_23. Obtuse, 153
_Y_24. Attrition, 155
_H_25. Eugenics, 156
_V_26. Extirpating, 206

A. State of being lustful
B. Two-footed creatures
C. Referring to diseases that recur
D. The act of sex
E. Of the study of languages and words
F. Beliefs that contradict orthodox beliefs
G. Something to relieve pain
H. Belief and practice of creating a desired human genetic outcome
I. Continually and forcefully urging
J. Greedy
K. Weak, without spirit
L. Lustful
M. Worthy of reward
N. Common, middle-class
O. Wipe out, destroy
P. Deviations from normal
Q. Cure-all
R. Discussed or debated
S. Stupid
T. Greed
U. Lifeless
V. Destroying, pulling up by the roots
W. Acts done for the good of others
X. Opposite
Y. The act of wearing out an opponent's men
Z. Purity

Two words hidden in vertical answers: <u>JACK LEWIS</u>

Lesson 9

Questions for Discussion

Teacher, before delving into the discussion questions, get things rolling with these:

1.   What questions do you have about *The Screwtape Letters*?
2.   What aspects of this book appealed to you?
3.   What is your impression of this book?

These preliminary questions will help to clear up any misunderstandings or miscomprehensions from the books, and they'll get students talking during the discussion session because they are open-ended questions. Students can answer other students' questions, too. This pre-discussion time may also serve to answer some of the questions printed below or can be a springboard to any of the aspects of the book you want to focus on.

1.   World War II was raging as Lewis wrote this book. Why do you think he doesn't mention it outright? *He did not want to date the book, to make it outdated in just a few years; he wanted it to have a more universal appeal.*
2.   Some of Screwtape's temptations are philosophical—trying to get the patient to believe something. Others are physical—urging the patient to do something. Which temptations in this book hit you the most? *Answers will vary.*
3.   "Humans are amphibians—half spirit and half animal" (37). Do you agree? Explain. *Answers will vary.*
4.   "All mortals tend to turn into the thing they are pretending to be" (50). Is this true? Explain. *Answers will vary.*
5.   "Every serious subject is discussed in a manner which implies that they have already found a ridiculous side to it" (56). Do you know anyone like that, who makes fun of everything or who makes even the most sacred things seem stupid or laughable? *Answers will vary.*
6.   Is Screwtape right when he writes that "a woman means by Unselfishness chiefly taking trouble for others; a man means not giving trouble to others" (142)? Give examples from characters in books and movies or from people you know. *Answers will vary.*
7.   Screwtape states that "only the physical facts are 'real' while the spiritual elements [of experiences] are 'subjective' " (168). To explain this concept, he says the sight of human entrails (the sight of someone who died violently) is simply a statement of Reality—that's the real world—but a light, happy emotion experienced while viewing happy children is simply sloppy sentiment, not real but subjective, a lazy man's way of escaping the "real"

178

world. This puts one in mind of the "scientific fact" that love is only a result of chemicals in the brain. Because this information about the "real" world is coming from the demon, we can assume it is untrue. What proofs can you give to show it is not true? *Answers will vary.*

8. Wormwood's patient is male. What temptations would Wormwood have employed had the patient been female? *Answers will vary.*

9. If you were in Wormwood's shoes, what physical, psychological, and philosophical temptations would you throw at the patient? *Answers will vary.*

10. Check out these verses. What do you learn about the devil in them?
    II Corinthians 2:11—The devil has schemes.
    II Corinthians 11:14—The devil masquerades as an angel of light.
    Ephesians 6:11-13—More schemes; our fight is not with humans but against principalities, powers, spiritual forces of evil. (II Corinthians 10:5—We also are fighting against arguments, ideas, and philosophies that set themselves "up against the knowledge of God," that keep people from knowing God.) We can arm ourselves against the devil's schemes.
    I Peter 5:8—Satan seeks to devour people.
    Romans 8:38-9—Demons cannot separate us from the love of God which is in Christ.

This is the end of lesson 9.

Your Choice of Activities

Note: Choose only one of the following activities. Read all of them carefully before you make your decision. Below you will find a short explanation of each activity. Your teacher will tell you when this is due.

- Be the Author—Write a letter.
- Be the Author II—Write a short story in letter form.
- The Artist in You—Depict the battle between good and evil.
- Create a Website—Create a Website for *The Screwtape Letters*.
- Compare and Contrast—Make lists comparing and contrasting demons and angels.
- Words and Music—Write a song.

Be the Author

Write your own letter from one demon to another or from one angel to a guardian angel. What advice will you give? What will your "younger" demon or angel need to know in order to be successful?

Be the Author II

As stated earlier, many fine novels are written in letter form. One interesting short story written with the letter device is "Marjorie Daw" by Thomas Bailey Aldrich. Aldrich chooses to have two men write back and forth to each other, and when things get heated up, they exchange telegrams. It is definitely a story with a twist.

Now is your chance to do the same. Write a short story comprised all in letters. You may choose to have the letters written by one person or by two people who are corresponding with one other. When you are finished, let someone read your masterpiece.

The Artist in You

Many famous artists have depicted the epic battle between good and evil. Stained glass, murals, and sculptures are just a few of the many ways artists can send a message or express an idea. Add your name to the famous list by using any medium you desire. If it is possible, enter your work in a contest or in a showing.

Create a Website

Where do people go to get information today? The Internet, of course. Create your own Website for *The Screwtape Letters* and for people who are interested in learning more about the book. What will you put on your site? What links will you include?

Compare and Contrast

The Bible has much to say about Satan and demons. Research the subject using a concordance; make a list of the things you learn. Then do the same thing with the subject of angels. Research the subject and make a list of the things you learn. When you have finished both lists, integrate them to show the comparisons and the contrasts between these unearthly beings.

Words and Music

There are some interesting songs written on the subject of the devil. George and Ira Gershwin wrote "It Ain't Necessarily So" (from *Porgy and Bess*), country singer Rodney Atkins penned "If You're Going Through Hell," Keith Green wrote "Lies," and Carman has an interesting song called "A Witch's Invitation" (https://www.youtube.com/watch?v=cJiheZ3aEug). No doubt you know of others. Try to find any of these songs or others on the topic, listen to them, and then write your own. Perform it before a friendly audience.

Teacher, you'll find the Grading Grid for *The Screwtape Letters* on the next page. The grid is marked for a possible 100 points per book. Please feel free to adjust it to your needs and expectations. You have permission to copy it as many times as needed for your own class, co-op, reading group, book-of-the-month club, or family.

180

Grading Grid for *The Screwtape Letters*

Student's Name: _____

Online "Yes, I read it" quiz, graded online. 1-10 points	
Online literary terms quiz, graded online. 1-10 points	
Participation in opinion questions online. 1-10 points	
Quality of participation in discussions. 1-20 points	
Successful completion of lessons and assignments. 1-20 points	
Successful completion of activity. 1-10 points	
Finished reading the book. 1-20 points.	
Total grade for *The Screwtape Letters*	

Writing with Sharon Watson

182

Endnotes

[1] Chuck Colson, "Pretty Stones and Dead Babies," BreakPoint.org, October 1, 2003, http://www.breakpoint.org/bpcommentaries/entry/13/11555.

[2] Lindsey Ziliak, "Finding your roots," *Kokomo Tribune*, January 26, 2013.

[3] Herbert George Wells, *Experiment in Autobiography: Discoveries and Conclusions of a Very Ordinary Brain (Since 1866)* (New York: The MacMillan Company, 1934), 131.

[4] Ibid., 457-8.

[5] Ibid., 44.

[6] Ibid.,70-1.

[7] Ibid., 46.

[8] Kurt Braunohler, "Best Laid Plans," moderated by Ira Glass, *This American Life*, Feb. 8, 2013, http://www.thisamericanlife.org/radio-archives/episode/486/valentines-day.

[9] Jessamyn West, *The Woman Said Yes* (New York: Harcourt, Brace. 1976), 52

[10] Andrew Birkin, *J. M. Barrie and the Lost Boys: The Real Story Behind Peter Pan* (London: Yale University Press, 2003).

[11] Susan Bivin Aller, *J. M. Barrie: The Magic Behind Peter Pan* (Minneapolis: Lerner Publications Company, 1994).

[12] http://www.jmbarrie.co.uk/, website copyright 2013 by Laurentic Wave Machine, accessed October 24, 2013.

[13] http://en.wikipedia.org/wiki/J._M._Barrie, Oct. 19, 2013 updated, Oct.25, 2013 accessed.

[14] www.raybradbury.com/at_home_clips.html#

Made in the USA
Lexington, KY
25 April 2017